Cambridge Primary

Computing

Learner's Book 1

Roland Birbal
Carissa Gookool
Michelle Koon Koon
Nazreen Mohammed
Michele Taylor

Series editor:
Roland Birbal

Although every effort has been made to ensure that website addresses are correct at time of going to press, Hodder Education cannot be held responsible for the content of any website mentioned in this book. It is sometimes possible to find a relocated web page by typing in the address of the home page for a website in the URL window of your browser.

Hachette UK's policy is to use papers that are natural, renewable and recyclable products and made from wood grown in well-managed forests and other controlled sources. The logging and manufacturing processes are expected to conform to the environmental regulations of the country of origin.

Orders: please contact Hachette UK Distribution, Hely Hutchinson Centre, Milton Road, Didcot, Oxfordshire, OX11 7HH. Telephone: +44 (0)1235 827827. Email education@hachette.co.uk. Lines are open from 9 a.m. to 5 p.m., Monday to Saturday, with a 24-hour message-answering service. You can also order through our website: www.hoddereducation.com

© Roland Birbal, Carissa Gookool, Michelle Koon Koon, Nazreen Mohammed, Michele Taylor 2022

First published in 2022 by
Hodder Education
An Hachette UK Company
Carmelite House
50 Victoria Embankment
London EC4Y 0DZ

www.hoddereducation.com

Impression number   10 9 8 7 6 5 4 3 2 1
Year   2026 2025 2024 2023 2022

All rights reserved. Apart from any use permitted under UK copyright law, no part of this publication may be reproduced or transmitted in any form or by any means, electronic or mechanical, including photocopying and recording, or held within any information storage and retrieval system, without permission in writing from the publisher or under licence from the Copyright Licensing Agency Limited. Further details of such licences (for reprographic reproduction) may be obtained from the Copyright Licensing Agency Limited, www.cla.co.uk

Cover illustration by Lisa Hunt from Bright Agency

Illustrations by Vian Oelofsen, Stéphan Theron, James Hearne

Typeset in FS Albert 17/19 by IO Publishing CC

Produced by DZS Grafik, Printed in Bosnia & Herzegovina

A catalogue record for this title is available from the British Library.

ISBN: 9781398368569

MIX
Paper | Supporting responsible forestry
FSC
www.fsc.org
FSC™ C104740

Contents

How to use this book

Get started! Talk about the new topic with a partner or small group.

You will learn: A list of things you will learn in the unit.

Get started!

Most of you have seen a computer or you may have one at home. The following pictures show different types of computers.

Discuss with your partner:
- Have you seen these computers before? Point to the pictures you have seen.
- What have you done on a computer?

In this unit, you will learn about different types of computers and the different things they can do.

You will learn:
- that computers can be used for different things
- that a computer can run different programs
- about data and information.

Warm up

1 Work in groups. Look at the three pictures below. Put them in the right order to tell a story. ____, ____, ____

Ⓐ   Ⓑ   Ⓒ   VS

2 Who will win the race?
☐ Turtle
☐ Rabbit
3 Now add the picture on the right.
Who will win the race now?
☐ Turtle
☐ Rabbit

Warm up: An offline activity to start your learning.

Do you remember?

Before starting this unit, check that you:
- can follow the steps in an algorithm
- know the order of steps is important
- know that algorithms are used to create code.

There is an online chapter about ScratchJr.

Do you remember? A list of things you should know before you start the unit.

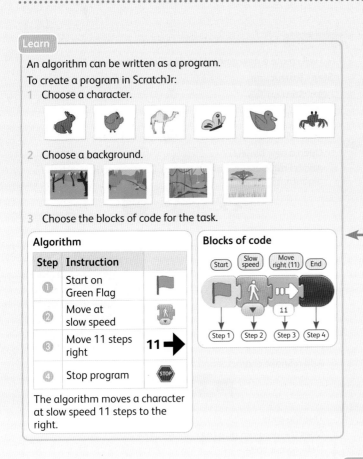

Learn

An algorithm can be written as a program.

To create a program in ScratchJr:

1 Choose a character.

2 Choose a background.

3 Choose the blocks of code for the task.

Algorithm

Step	Instruction	
1	Start on Green Flag	
2	Move at slow speed	
3	Move 11 steps right	11➡
4	Stop program	STOP

Blocks of code

The algorithm moves a character at slow speed 11 steps to the right.

Learn: Learn new computing skills with your teacher. Look at the instructions to help you.

Practise

Practise: Answer questions to learn more and practise your new skills.

1 Open the game from page 136.

2 Here is a new algorithm for the **Frog**. This is the new result we want in the game.

Step	Instruction	
1	Start on Tap	
2	Jump 8 grid squares	
3	Say "Ribbit"	
4	Stop program	STOP

3 Here is the new code for the **Frog**:

4 Change your program to the new code for the **Frog**. Test this code.

5 We want to add a **Snake** to the game. Here is the algorithm for the **Snake**.

Step	Instruction	
1	Start on Green Flag	
2	Play Pop sound	POP
3	Move 6 steps right	6➡
4	Stop program	STOP

6 Select a **Snake** character.

7 Create the code to match the algorithm.

8 Test your program. Did you get the right result?

Go further: Activities to make you think carefully about computing.

You will create a new game. Here is an algorithm for a **Frog**:

Step	Instruction	
1	Start on Tap	🖐
2	Turn right (5)	5 ↱
3	Stop program	STOP

1 Open a new project.
2 Add a **Frog** character and this code. Does the code match the algorithm?

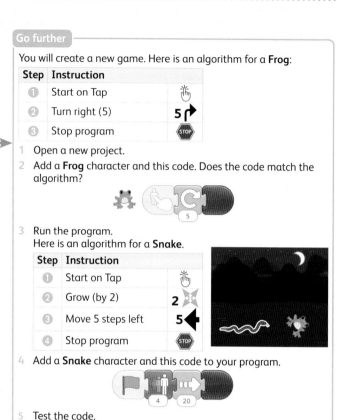

3 Run the program.
Here is an algorithm for a **Snake**.

Step	Instruction	
1	Start on Tap	🖐
2	Grow (by 2)	2
3	Move 5 steps left	5 ◀
4	Stop program	STOP

4 Add a **Snake** character and this code to your program.

5 Test the code.
6 Does the program give the right result?
7 Debug your code.

Using your game from the last page:
1 Add the **Bat** character.

Adventure game

2 Add code to the **Bat**.
The code should match this algorithm.

Step	Instruction	
1	Start on Green Message	✉
2	Move 1 step up	1 ▲
3	Stop program	STOP

3 Draw a **Green Button** using the **Paint Editor**.
4 Add code to the **Green Button** to match this algorithm:

Step	Instruction	
1	Start on Tap	🖐
2	Send Green Start Message	✉
3	Stop program	STOP

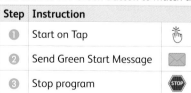

The **Green Button** controls the **Frog**.

5 Test your program. Does it give the right result?
6 If not, check for errors and correct them.

Challenge yourself! A harder activity to test your new skills.

All links to additional resources can be found at: https://www.hoddereducation.co.uk/cambridgeextras

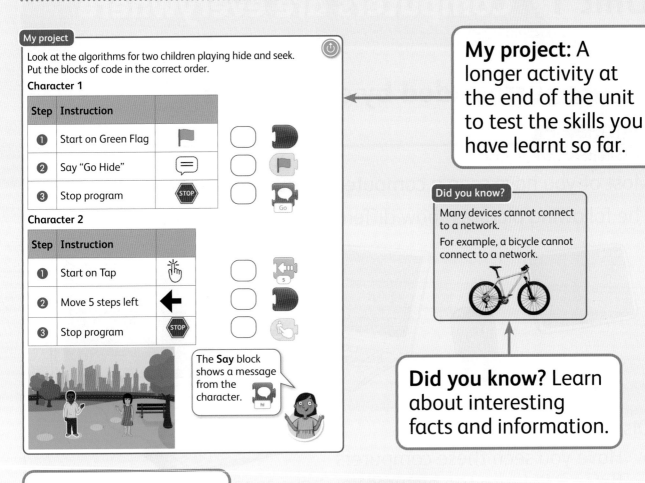

My project

Look at the algorithms for two children playing hide and seek. Put the blocks of code in the correct order.

Character 1

Step	Instruction		
❶	Start on Green Flag	🚩	◯
❷	Say "Go Hide"	💬	◯
❸	Stop program	STOP	◯

Character 2

Step	Instruction		
❶	Start on Tap	👆	◯
❷	Move 5 steps left	◀	◯
❸	Stop program	STOP	◯

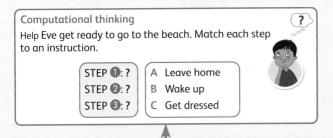

The **Say** block shows a message from the character.

My project: A longer activity at the end of the unit to test the skills you have learnt so far.

Did you know?

Many devices cannot connect to a network.

For example, a bicycle cannot connect to a network.

Did you know? Learn about interesting facts and information.

What can you do? Find out how much you have learnt and what you can do.

What can you do?

Read and review what you can do.
- ✔ I know what an algorithm is.
- ✔ I can follow the steps in an algorithm.
- ✔ I know an algorithm can be created as code.

Great job! Now you know how to follow algorithms and code!

Computational thinking

Help Eve get ready to go to the beach. Match each step to an instruction.

STEP ❶: ?   A Leave home
STEP ❷: ?   B Wake up
STEP ❸: ?   C Get dressed

Computational thinking: A task that tests your computational thinking skills.

Keywords

algorithm: a set of instructions for a task or problem
instructions: information about how something should be done
task: an activity

Keywords: Understand new computing words. The **Glossary** at the end of the book also lists all of these words.

We are surrounded by computers

Get started!

Most of you have seen a computer or you may have one at home. The following pictures show different types of computers.

Discuss with your partner:

- Have you seen these computers before? Point to the pictures you have seen.
- What have you done on a computer?

 In this unit, you will learn about different types of computers and the different things they can do.

You will learn:

- that computers can be used for different things
- that a computer can run different programs
- about data and information.

Warm up

1   Work in pairs. Can you name the parts of this computer system?

2   Discuss with your partner:
*   What is a computer?
*   What can you do on a computer?

Do you remember?

Before starting this unit, check that you:
*   know your letter sounds.

What is a computer?

Learn

A computer is a machine that can:
- take in data
- do something to the data
- give a result.

A computer cannot think for itself.

A computer will do exactly as it is told.

Computers can be found everywhere. For example, there are computers in:
- Supermarkets
- Hospitals
- Schools
- Cars.

There are different types of computers.

Keyword

data: numbers, words, pictures, sounds or videos

A desktop computer has a:

monitor

tower

keyboard

mouse

You cannot carry it around.

A laptop is smaller than a desktop.
You can carry it around easily.

A tablet is smaller than a laptop.

You can carry it around.

It can do many things a laptop can.

It has a touchscreen.

A smartphone is a small computer.
It can make phone calls.
It is smaller than a tablet.
You can carry it around.
It can do many things a tablet can.
It has a touchscreen.

Which type of computer is the easiest to carry around?

Practise

1   Match each word to each picture.

(tablet)   (desktop)   (smartphone)   (laptop)

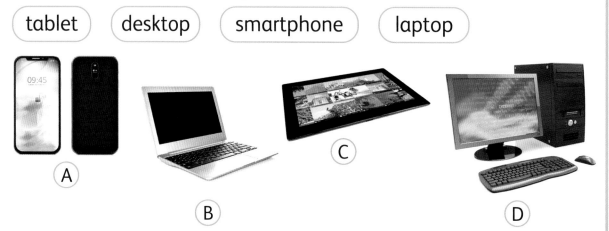

2   Which computer is the largest?

3   Which computer is the smallest?

Work in groups of four.

4   Discuss which of these devices are computers:

5   Count the number of **laptops** in the pictures below.

6   Count the number of **smartphones** in the pictures below.

Did you know?

We use computers every day.

Can you name some of the places you have seen computers?

What do we use computers for?

Learn

Computers can do many different things.

We use computers:

For fun:

We can play games, listen to music and watch movies.

To talk or message:

We can talk to our friends and family.

To make things:

We can draw and design things on the computer.

To find out things:

We can search for information about anything.

Computer programs

To do different things, a computer uses different programs.

Programs are also known as apps.

Programs tell the computer what to do.

Different programs do different things.

Keywords

program: instructions for the computer to follow

app: this is another name for a program

For fun:

There are programs to watch videos or play a game.

To talk or message:

There are programs to make video calls or chat.

To make things:

There are programs to draw and paint pictures.

To find out things:

There are programs that let us search.

I use the computer to play games. What do you use the computer to do?

What type of apps do you use on your computer?

Practise

Work in groups of four.

1 Can you identify the software below and what they are used for?

A   B   C   D   E

(paint a picture)   (play a game)   (watch a video)

(search)   (chat)

2 Match the tasks below to the pictures. Write the letter next to the task. One has been done for you.

(D Watching movies)   (◯ Playing music)   (◯ Talking to friends)

(◯ Sending a letter)   (◯ Playing a game)   (◯ Doing schoolwork)

3   Match the activity with the program.
Write the number of the activity and the letter of the program.

1 For writing: We can write letters using our computers.

2 For learning: We can learn about things using computers.

3 For school: We can use programs to access school work.

4 For coding: We can write programs using computers.

5 For games: We can play games using computers.

A
Google Classroom

B
ScratchJr

C
Khan Academy Kids*

D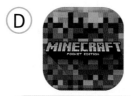
Minecraft

E
Microsoft Word

*Khan Academy Kids is a free educational app for children ages 2–8.
Learn more at www.khankids.org.

Input devices

Learn

Input devices let you put data into a computer.

The type of input device depends on the type of data.

Data can be numbers, words, pictures, sounds or videos.

A mouse is used to select things on the screen. 	A keyboard is used to input letters and words. 
A microphone is used to input sound. 	A webcam is used to input video. 

Did you know?

Some apps can turn speech into written words.

Practise

1 Circle all the input devices in the picture.

How many did you find?

2 Match the following pictures to the type of information they put into the computer.

Device		Input	

Go further

Computers are found inside other devices. They control what the device does.

1 Fill in the blanks using words from the word bank.

(mouse) (video camcorder) (keyboard) (camera) (microphone)

a I can use a _____ to type a letter.

b I take pictures with this device: _____.

c My _____ can record a video of my

birthday party.

d This _____ allows me to record my rap song.

e I use a _____ to move the pointer on the

computer screen.

2 Match the sentences to the apps.

a I use ⊙ to watch videos.

b I use W to write a letter.

c I use 🐱 to write computer programs.

d I use to play a game.

(ScratchJr)

(Minecraft)

(Microsoft Word)

(An online video service)

Challenge yourself!

Work in groups.

1 Find all the types of computers in the room. How many did you find?

2 Name the types of computers that you found.

3 Which computers are easy to carry around?

My project

1   Find or draw some pictures of the different types of computers that you have learnt about.

> You can choose from a:
> - desktop computer
> - laptop
> - tablet
> - smartphone.

Create a scrapbook using your images or drawings. You can have more than one picture for each type of computer.

2   Talk to one of your classmates about:

   a   some of the things you can use a computer for

   b   the programs you would use.

What can you do?

Read and review what you can do.

✔ I know that computers can be used for different things.

✔ I know that computers can use different programs.

✔ I know about data and information.

✔ I know about input devices.

Great work! Now you know how computers are used.

Unit 2 Be an animator

Completing tasks

Get started!

Work in small groups.

Describe how you get ready for school.
Take turns to show what you do.

- What is the order of each activity?
- Do you do the same activities every day?

You will learn:

- what an algorithm is
- to follow the steps in an algorithm
- that algorithms can be created as code.

In this unit, you will create algorithms and understand code from ScratchJr.

Warm up

Get the monkey to the banana.

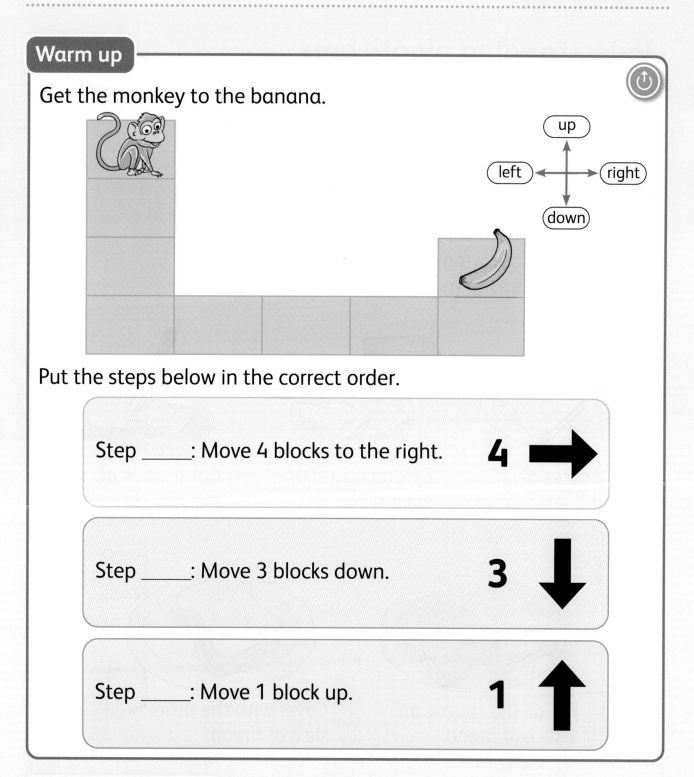

Put the steps below in the correct order.

Step _____: Move 4 blocks to the right. 4 ➡

Step _____: Move 3 blocks down. 3 ⬇

Step _____: Move 1 block up. 1 ⬆

Do you remember?

Before starting this unit, check that you can:
•   think of some everyday tasks.

Understanding algorithms
Following steps

Learn

An everyday task is something a person does each day.
Examples are eating, walking and getting dressed.

Follow the steps for an everyday task
One everyday task is making a sandwich.
Here are the steps to make a cheese sandwich.

1

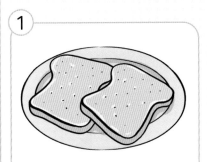

Get 2 slices of bread.

2

Spread butter on each slice.

3

Cut 4 slices of cheese.

4

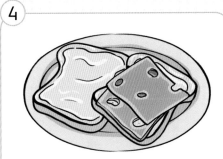

Put all the cheese on 1 slice of bread.

5

Cover with the other slice of bread.

We follow the steps in the right order to complete a task.

1   The steps below are for washing hands.
    What is the right order of steps? The first two are done for you.
    Steps: A, C, ___, ___, ___

| A | Wet hands with water. |  |

| B | Rinse soap from hands with water. |  |

| C | Get soap. |  |

| D | Dry hands. |  |

| E | Scrub hands. |  |

2   Show your partner how you would follow these steps.

Writing algorithms

An algorithm is a set of instructions. Algorithms are used to carry out a task or solve a problem.

The steps to make a cheese sandwich are an example of an algorithm.

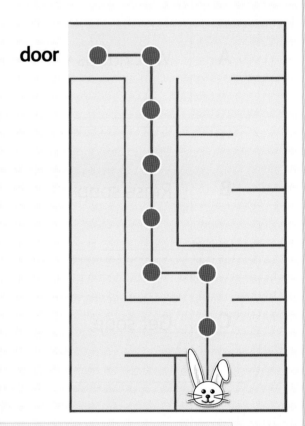

door

Keywords

algorithm: a set of instructions for a task or problem

instructions: information about how something should be done

task: an activity

Algorithm for solving a problem

The instructions below are for a maze.
The instructions tell the rabbit how to get to the door.

Step	Instruction		
1	Move 2 steps up	🐰	2 ⬆
2	Move 1 step left	🐰	1 ⬅
3	Move 4 steps up	🐰	4 ⬆
4	Move 1 step left	🐰	1 ⬅

Practise

Algorithm for completing a task

Here is an algorithm to walk around a table from Start to End.

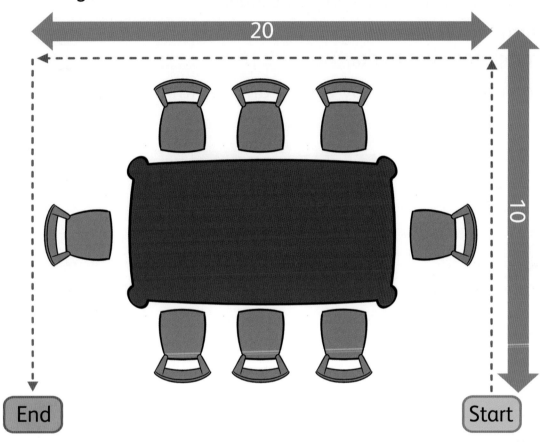

Put the steps in the right order. The first one is done for you.

Steps: 3, ___, ___

Step	Instruction		
①	Walk 20 steps left	**20** ←
②	Walk 10 steps down	**10** ↓
③	Walk 10 steps up	**10** ↑

This algorithm has a total of 3 steps.

Creating code

Programs are instructions for computers.

Programs are written using code. Code is a special language that tells the computer what to do.

We can plan a program by writing an algorithm.

This algorithm moves the **Driver** character to the right:

Step	Instruction	
①	Start on Green Flag	
②	Move 5 steps right	**5** ➡
③	Stop program	STOP

The 3 steps in the algorithm can be created as 3 blocks of code.

In ScratchJr, we join the blocks together.

The complete code will look like this:

Keywords

code: commands that tell a computer what to do

program: a set of code that completes a task

Practise

1   This algorithm moves the **Driver** 10 steps left. Put the steps in the correct order: Steps: ___, ___, ___

Step	Instruction	
A	Stop program	
B	Move 10 steps left	
C	Start on Green Flag	

2   Each block of code matches one step in the algorithm.

Match the blocks to the steps. The first one has been done for you.

Step 1: **C**

Step 2: ___

Step 3: ___

Step 4: ___

① Start on Green Flag

② Shrink size by 2

③ Move 10 steps up

④ Stop program

Ⓐ

Ⓑ

Ⓒ

Ⓓ

Groups of blocks in ScratchJr have different colours.

Go further

Eve is going to the beach.

Computational thinking

Help Eve get ready to go to the beach. Match each step to an instruction.

STEP ❶: ?	A Leave home
STEP ❷: ?	B Wake up
STEP ❸: ?	C Get dressed

1   At the beach, Eve moves 7 steps to the right. Then she jumps up 2 steps. The steps in the algorithm are in the wrong order. Put the steps in the right order. The first one has been done for you.

Step	Instruction	
	Jump up 2 steps	🧍
❶	Start on Green Flag	🚩
	Stop program	🛑
	Move 7 steps right	**7** ➡

Hint: You can use the **Hop** block to jump.

2   Choose the correct pair of blocks to match the algorithm in question **1**.

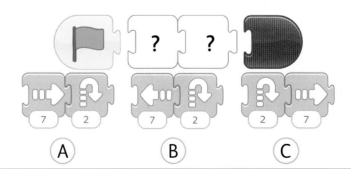

A   B   C

Challenge yourself!

Eve goes searching for shells. She follows the path shown.

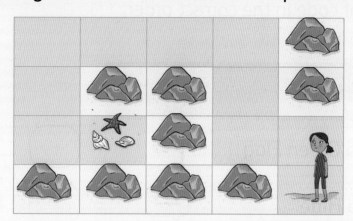

1   Copy and complete the steps for the algorithm that follows this path.

Step	Instruction	
1	Start on Tap	🖱
	Move 1 step left	1 ←
	Move 2 steps up	2 ↑
2	Move 1 step up	1 ↑
5	Move 3 steps left	3 ←
8	Stop program	🛑 STOP
7	Move 1 step right	1 →
	Move 2 steps down	2 ↓

You can use the **Start on Tap** block to start the program when you tap a character.

My project

Look at the algorithms for two children playing hide and seek.
Put the blocks of code in the correct order.

Character 1

Step	Instruction	
❶	Start on Green Flag	🚩
❷	Say "Go Hide"	💬
❸	Stop program	STOP

Character 2

Step	Instruction	
❶	Start on Tap	👆
❷	Move 5 steps left	⬅
❸	Stop program	STOP

The **Say** block shows a message from the character.

Did you know?

Algorithms are everywhere:
- The steps to brush your teeth are an algorithm.
- The instructions to make a cake are an algorithm.
- Computer games use many different algorithms.

What can you do?

Read and review what you can do.
- ✔ I know what an algorithm is.
- ✔ I can follow the steps in an algorithm.
- ✔ I know an algorithm can be created as code.

Great job! Now you know how to follow algorithms and code!

Understanding data

Get started!

Each picture below shows a computing device.

1 Tell your friend the name of each device.
   Use the words below to help you.

(games console) (sales terminal) (smartphone) (smartwatch)

2 What can you see on each device?

You will learn:

• that computing devices can answer questions

• that computing devices can sort data

• that computing devices can organise data.

In this unit, you will learn about data and how to sort and organise it.

Warm up

Work in pairs. You will need paper and crayons.

1 Write these letters on a sheet of paper. Write each letter in the colour shown.

A Z C A
C M A C
T A H W
H G D L

2 Write the letters again but group them by colour. Here is how to group all of the blue letters: C A T H

3 a How many letters are blue?
   b How many letters are red?
   c How many letter Cs are there?
   d How many letters are green?

Do you remember?

Before starting this unit, check that you:
- can say the alphabet
- can count from 1 to 10
- can identify shapes and colours.

Managing data
Asking questions

Keyword
computing device: a machine that works with data

Computing devices can answer many questions.
Computing devices can answer questions such as:
- what is the weather like?
- what time is the bus?

Here are some questions computing devices are often asked:

Supermarket	How much is this item?	
Library	Do you have a copy of this book?	
Games	Who has the highest score?	

Remember, data can be numbers, words, pictures, sounds or videos.

Practise

Work in pairs to answer the questions.

1 a Which device is used to check the weather?
   b Which device is used in supermarkets?
   c Which device can count how many steps you have walked?

smartwatch

smartphone

sales terminal

2 Here are some computing devices.

fitness tracker

tablet

laptop

   a Which device can tell you your heart rate?
   b Which devices can tell the time?

Sorting data

Keyword

sort: to group items or data that have something in common

Learn

Look at the picture. Can you easily count the number of green blocks?

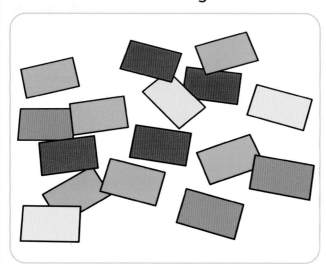

To count the blocks, we can sort them by colour.

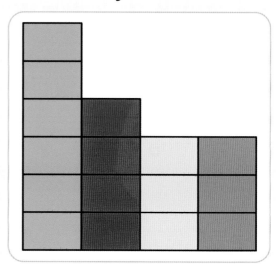

Sorting means grouping things together. For example, grouping by colour or size.

Computers can also sort data. You can know more about data if it is sorted.

These two pictures show data on a computer:

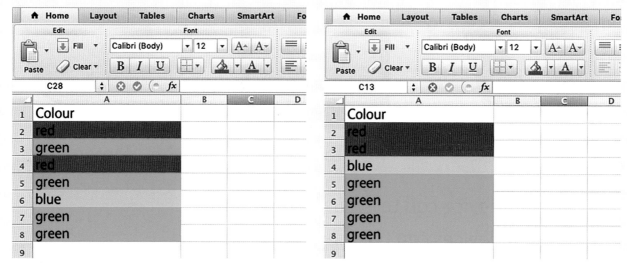

Point to the picture that you think has sorted data.

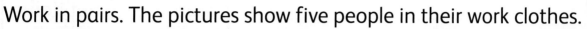

Practise

Work in pairs. The pictures show five people in their work clothes.

Your teacher will give you a copy of this table.

Fill the table with each person's data.

The first one is done for you.

Job	Man or woman	Hat or no hat	Coat or no coat
firefighter	man	hat	coat
carpenter			
doctor			
chef			
dentist			

Let us sort the people in the table.

1 How many people are men? Shade the boxes with the word 'man' in blue.

2 How many people are women? Shade the boxes with the word 'woman' in red.

3 How many people wear hats? Shade the boxes with the word 'hat' in yellow.

4 How many people wear coats? Shade the boxes with the word 'coat' in green.

Organising data

Learn

Look at the first picture.

Who is the tallest child? Who is the shortest?

Look at the second picture. Point to the tallest and shortest child.

It is easier to see who is shortest in the second picture. The children are in order from shortest to tallest.

Computers can put data in order. When data is in order it is organised.

Numbers can be put in order from smallest to largest.

Numbers
1
2
3
4
5

Letters can be put in order from a to z.

Letters
a
b
c
d
e

Numbers can be put in order from largest to smallest.

Numbers
5
4
3
2
1

Letters can be put in order from z to a.

Letters
e
d
c
b
a

Practise

Your teacher will give you a copy of the tables to fill in.

In each table put the data in order.

1 a Write the numbers from smallest to largest.

 b Write the numbers from largest to smallest.

Number	Smallest to largest	Largest to smallest
8		
10		
7		
9		

2 a Write the letters in order from j to m.

 b Write the letters in order from m to j.

Letters	From j to m	From m to j
k		
m		
l		
j		

Go further

Zara would like to visit the pizza shop.

1 a **What device can Zara use to find the pizza shop?**

tablet

sales terminal

   b **Why did you choose that answer?**

2 Zara wants to order a pizza.
   The options are:
   - small, medium, large
   - circle, rectangle
   - meat, vegetarian

   a 'Sort' means to group. What are TWO ways to sort the pizzas?
   b 'Organise' means to put in order. Draw the pizzas in order of size.

Did you know?

Pizza shops use data to keep track of their pizza orders.

★ Challenge yourself!

1   Your teacher will give you a copy of this picture. Circle all
    the computing devices.

2   Look at these houses.

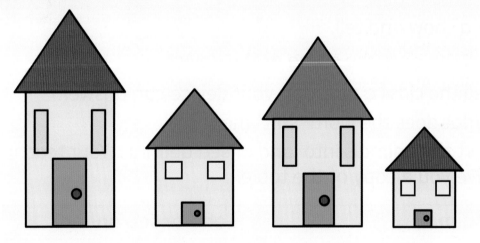

a   What are TWO ways to sort the houses?

b   Draw the houses from smallest to largest.

Remember, 'sort'
means to group.

My project

1 Work in groups. Choose one of these computing devices:

smartwatch   laptop   fitness tracker

smartphone   tablet

Have a show and tell.

• Tell the class the name of the device.

• Tell the class a question your device can answer.

2 a What does the word 'sort' mean?

   b Sort the animals into land or sea animals. Your teacher will
      give you a copy of the table.

Animal	Land or sea animal
fish	
cat	
whale	
horse	

3 a What does 'organise' mean?

   b Your teacher will give you a copy of the table.
      In the table write the numbers:

      • from smallest to largest
      • from largest to smallest

Number	Small to large	Large to small
4		
3		
5		

What can you do?

Read and review what you can do.

✔ I know that computing devices can answer questions.

✔ I know computers can sort data.

✔ I know computers can put data in order.

Great job! Now you know that computers can answer questions, sort and organise data.

Be a designer

Designing to create

Get started!

Work in pairs. Tell your partner what you would build with blocks.

Draw your idea on paper and compare it with your partner.

Can you change your drawing?

Change your drawing to make something new.

You will learn:

- how to change algorithms
- to create programs in ScratchJr
- to tell what happens when you run a program.

In this unit, you will learn how to change algorithms, and create programs in ScratchJr.

Warm up

1   Work in groups. Look at the three pictures below. Put them in the right order to tell a story. ____, ____, ____

2   Who will win the race?

☐ Turtle
☐ Rabbit

3   Now add the picture on the right.

Who will win the race now?

☐ Turtle
☐ Rabbit

Do you remember?

Before starting this unit, check that you:
*   can follow the steps in an algorithm
*   know that the order of steps is important
*   know that algorithms are used to create code.

There is an online chapter about ScratchJr.

Algorithms
Changing the outcome

An algorithm is a set of instructions.

Changing the instructions can change the outcome.

Look at the algorithm below for the rabbit.

This rabbit must move:

- at a slow speed
- 11 steps right.

> **Keyword**
> **outcome**: result

Algorithm

Step	Instruction	
1	Start on Green Flag	
2	Move at slow speed	
3	Move 11 steps right	**11** →
4	Stop program	STOP

Let us change the algorithm so the rabbit moves faster.

New algorithm

In the new algorithm, the rabbit moves faster.

Step	Instruction	
1	Start on Green Flag	🚩
2	Move at fast speed	
3	Move 11 steps right	**11** ➡
4	Stop program	STOP

Changing the algorithm changes the outcome.

This algorithm moves a rocket at fast speed.

Step	Instruction	
①	Start on Green Flag	🚩
②	Move at fast speed	
③	Move 9 steps up	9 ⬆
④	Stop program	STOP

1   Change the algorithm so the rocket moves at a slow speed.

What is the new speed of the rocket?

⬜ slow   ⬜ fast

2   We want the rocket to move higher. How many steps should the rocket move up?

⬜ 5 steps   ⬜ 12 steps

Programs in ScratchJr

An algorithm can be written as a program.

To create a program in ScratchJr:

1 Choose a character.

2 Choose a background.

3 Choose the blocks of code for the task.

Algorithm

Step	Instruction	
①	Start on Green Flag	🏳
②	Move at slow speed	
③	Move 11 steps right	**11**➡
④	Stop program	STOP

The algorithm moves a character at slow speed 11 steps to the right.

Blocks of code

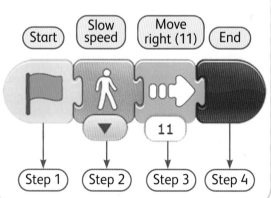

Practise

Let us create a program for a rabbit to:

- move at medium speed
- move to the rock.

1 Open ScratchJr.

2 Add the **Rabbit** character.

3 Add the background above.

Did you know that you can take a photo using the **Camera** tool? The photo can be used as a background.

Algorithm for Rabbit

Step	Instruction	
1	Start on Green Flag	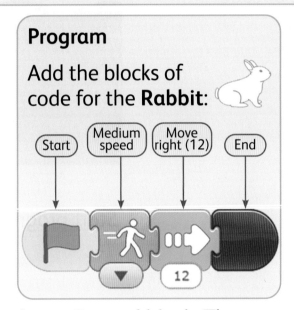
2	Move at medium speed	
3	Move 12 steps right	**12**
4	Stop program	STOP

Program

Add the blocks of code for the **Rabbit**:

Start · Medium speed · Move right (12) · End

The **Set Speed** block is a **Control** block. There are 3 speeds – slow, medium and fast.

Slow   Medium   Fast

Click on the Green Flag to start the program.

The **Rabbit** moves at medium speed to the rock.

Predicting outcomes of programs

Learn

The outcome of a program can be guessed.

We can do this by looking at each block of code.

We need to understand each block of code.

Program for plane	Instruction
Look at the blocks of code below for a plane.	
	① Start program on Green Flag
	② Move at **fast** speed
	③ Move 11 steps up
	④ Stop program

The plane moves at fast speed.

The plane moves 11 steps up.

Practise

Look at these blocks of code. The **Dog**, **Chicken** and **Rabbit** characters have a race.

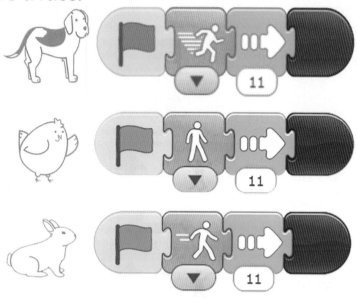

1   Guess the results of the race.

Animal	Guess	Result
Dog		
Chicken		
Rabbit		

2   Add this code in ScratchJr. Run your program to see what happens.

3   Did you guess right?

4   What would happen if the direction block for **Chicken** is changed to this?

Change the block and run your program.

Go further

This algorithm shows Jamie's dance moves.

Step	Instruction		Block of code
①	Start on Green Flag	🏳	
②	Move at slow speed		
③	Hop 4 steps up	4 ⬆	
④	Move 2 steps right	2 ➡	
⑤	Hop 6 steps up	6 ⬆	
⑥	Stop program	STOP	

1   Jamie wants to jump even higher.

   Which steps in the algorithm need to be changed?

2   Match each block of code with the step in the algorithm.

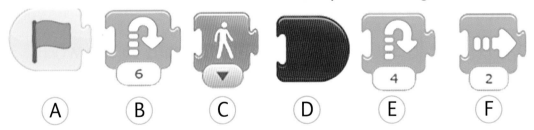

   A   B   C   D   E   F

3   Change the speed block to:

   Will Jamie dance faster or slower?
   Run the program. Did you guess correctly?

⭐ Challenge yourself!

Look at this algorithm for a **Seahorse** character.

Step	Instruction	
①	Start on Green Flag	🚩
②	Move at medium speed	
③	Move 6 steps up	**6** ⬆
④	Stop program	STOP

1 This code should match the algorithm. Put the blocks of code in order.

Block of code				
Algorithm step		1		

We want the **Seahorse** to move faster.

2 How fast should the **Seahorse** now move?

   a Slow   b Medium   c Fast

   Here is a new program for the **Seahorse**:

3 Will the **Seahorse**:

   ☐ Move at fast speed 3 steps right?

   ☐ Move at slow speed 3 steps right?

Computational thinking

Frank moves fast for 13 steps to the right.

He then slows down and goes 3 steps left.

Ⓐ   Ⓑ   Ⓒ   Ⓓ   Ⓔ   Ⓕ

Arrange the blocks of code in the correct order.

Step	Letter
①	A
②	
③	
④	
⑤	
⑥	B

My project

Work in groups.

Create a program for a boat to sail.

1 Open ScratchJr.

2 Choose a background like this:

3 Choose the **Boat** character.

4 This algorithm is for the **Boat** to sail.

Step	Instruction	
❶	Start on Green Flag	⚑
❷	Move at slow speed	
❸	Move 14 steps right	14 ➡
❹	Stop program	STOP

Choose the correct blocks of code to match the algorithm.

(A)   (B)   (C)   (D)   (E)

5 Add the blocks of code in ScratchJr.

6 Run the program to see what happens.

7 What will happen if this block:

is used instead of this block?

Did you know?

Ada Lovelace is known as the first computer programmer.

She wrote the first algorithm to be carried out by a computer.

She wrote this algorithm in 1843!

What can you do?

Read and review what you can do.

✔ I can change an algorithm.

✔ I can create algorithms as programs in ScratchJr.

✔ I can tell what happens when I run a program.

Awesome work! You are now a Program Designer!

Networks and the internet

Get started!

Talk with your partner:

- Who is in your family?
- Do you talk to your family?
- Does your family talk to each other?

Your family are connected together to form a family network.

Computers can also connect to form networks.

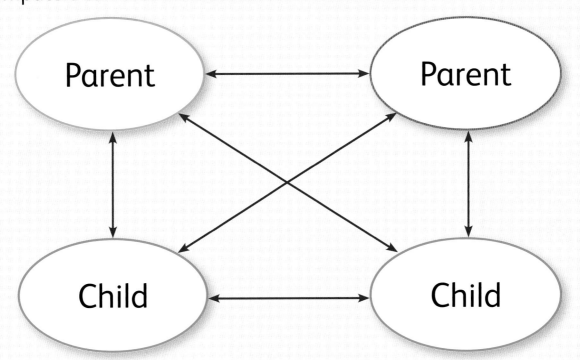

You will learn:

- about networks
- about the internet.

In this unit, you will learn about networks and the internet.

Warm up

1   Form three circles with everyone in the class.
2   Pass a note around the first circle. The note can only pass to people next to each other.
3   Can you pass the note to the second circle?
4   Join circles 1 and 2 to form the number '8'.
5   Now can you pass the note to a person in the second circle?
6   What can you do to pass the note to the third circle?

Do you remember?

Before starting this unit, check that you:
•   know the meaning of the word 'data'
•   know the meaning of the word 'information'
•   know what software is.

Networks
What is a network?

Learn

Two or more computers can connect together.

When computers connect together, it is called a network.

Computers in a network let you communicate.

You can send emails and text messages to your friends.

Computers in a network can share devices.

A printer can connect to a network. Any computer in the network can use the printer.

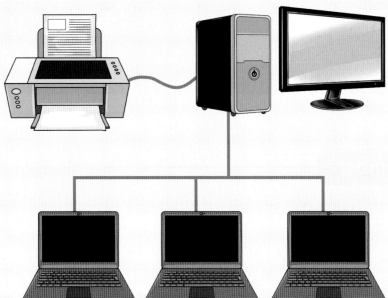

Computers in a network can share things like photographs.

Photographs on one computer can be shared with another computer in the network.

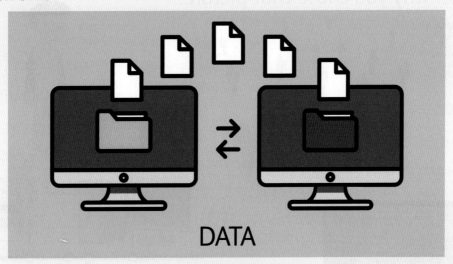

Computers in a network can share software.

This lets students use the same software during class.

Software is another name for a program.

Keywords

network: two or more computers connected together

communicate: share information, news, or ideas

device: printers, mice and keyboards are all examples of devices

Practise

1   Point to the picture that shows a network of people. Tell your partner why you chose that picture.

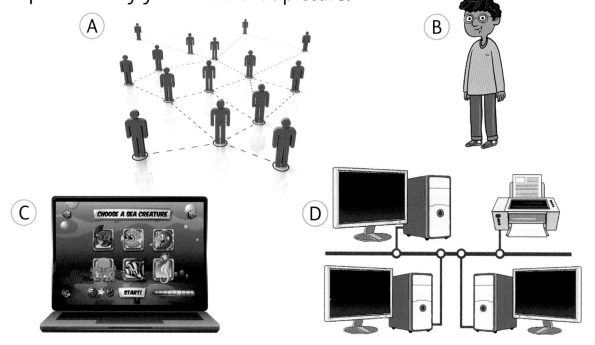

2   Point to the picture that shows a network of computers. Tell your partner why you chose that picture.

Network devices

Several devices can connect to a network.

A desktop computer can connect to a network.

A laptop can connect to a network.

A laptop is easier to move than a desktop computer.

A smartphone can connect to a network.

People use smartphones to communicate and share information.

A tablet can connect to a network.

A tablet is a small, flat computer with a touchscreen.

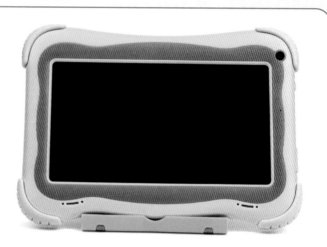

A smartwatch can connect to a network.

A smartwatch is a computer that looks like a watch.

A smartwatch can do many things a smartphone can do.

Did you know?

Many devices cannot connect to a network.

For example, a bicycle cannot connect to a network.

What other devices cannot connect to a network?

Practise

1   Say each word and show your partner the correct device.

smartphone   printer   tablet   laptop

2   Point to the devices that can connect to a network. Tell your partner why you chose those devices.

3   Point to the devices that cannot be part of a network. Tell your partner why you chose those devices.

Internet
What is the internet?

Learn

The internet is the largest computer network in the world.

Lots of computers are connected to the internet.

The internet connects computers and devices around the world.

You can share pictures on the internet.

You can chat with your friends on the internet.

You can play games with friends on the internet.

What other things can you do on the internet?

Practise

1 Read the statements and say if they are true or false.

a   The internet is one computer.
    True   False

b   Two computers connected together is called the internet.
    True   False

c   The internet is lots of computers connected around the world.
    True   False

d   The internet is a place.
    True   False

e   I can share information on the internet.
    True   False

f   I can chat with friends on the internet.
    True   False

g   I can send pictures to my friends on the internet.
    True   False

h   I cannot play games with my friends on the internet.
    True   False

Go further

1 True or false?

		True	False
a	Two laptops can connect to a network.		
b	A laptop and a desktop can connect to a network.		
c	A network only includes computers.		
d	A tablet and a laptop connected together is a network.		
e	A laptop, a desktop and a printer connected together is a network.		
f	The internet is the largest computer network in the world.		
g	All devices can connect to the internet.		

2 Talk to your partner. What can you do with a smartphone when connected to the internet?

3 You and your family are on vacation in Bangkok. You want to send pictures to friends in London.

Tell your partner how you can send the pictures.

⭐ Challenge yourself!

1. Draw a picture of a network.
   a. Tell your partner the names of the devices you added.
   b. Tell your partner what the devices can do.
   c. Tell your partner what you can share on a network.
2. What devices can you add to a network?
3. Draw a picture of what you think the internet looks like.

My project

Using playdough, make a model of a network with your partner.

Tell your partner the name of each device in your network.

Tell your partner some of the things you can do on the internet.

What can you do?

Read and review what you can do.

✔ I know what a network is.

✔ I know what the internet is.

Fantastic job – now you know about networks and the internet.

Solving problems

Get started!

Work in pairs. Show your partner how you brush your teeth.
What steps do you take?

You will learn:

- to find errors in an algorithm
- to put instructions in the right order
- that programs can have errors.

In this unit, you will write algorithms and programs in ScratchJr.

Warm up

Work in small groups. Look at the pictures below.
They show the steps for baking a cake.

A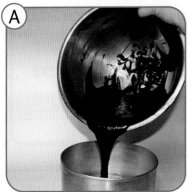

B

The pictures are not in order.

C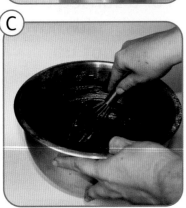

D

STEP **1**: ?

STEP **2**: ?

STEP **3**: ?

STEP **4**: ?

Put the pictures in the right order.

Do you remember?

Before starting this unit, check that you:
* can change an algorithm
* can guess what will happen when you run a program.

There is an online chapter all about ScratchJr.

Understanding errors
Finding errors in algorithms

Learn

Algorithms may not work if there is an error.
Algorithm for sunset
The algorithms below are for a sunset.
There is an error in the first algorithm.
The error is the direction the sun moves.

Keyword
error: a mistake in an algorithm or program

Incorrect algorithm

Step	Instruction	
1	Start on Green Flag	⚑
2	Move 3 steps (up)	3 ⬆
3	Hide sun	✖
4	Stop program	STOP

For a sunset, the sun should move **down not up**.

Correct algorithm

Step	Instruction	
1	Start on Green Flag	⚑
2	Move 3 steps down	3 ⬇
3	Hide sun	✖
4	Stop program	STOP

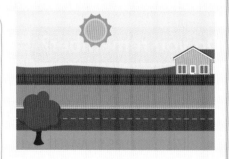

Practise

1 Find the error in each algorithm below.

Algorithm 1 – The Moon
The Moon has to move 2 steps up .

Step	Instruction	
1	Start on Green Flag	🏳
2	Move 2 steps down	**2** ⬇
3	Stop program	STOP

Algorithm 2 – The Driver
The car has to move 4 steps left.

Step	Instruction	
1	Start on Green Flag	🏳
2	Move 6 steps left	**6** ⬅
3	Stop program	STOP

2 Fill in the blanks in this algorithm.

Algorithm 3 – The Sun
We want the **Sun** to
- move 8 steps right
- move 3 steps down

Step	Instruction	
1	Start on Green Flag	🏳
2	Move _____	
3	Move _____	
4	Go to next page	

Ordering instructions

Learn

The steps in an algorithm need to be in the right order.

Algorithm for making pizza

Here are two algorithms for making a pizza.

- In Algorithm A, cheese is added after cooking the pizza. The pizza will not taste great!
- In Algorithm B, cheese is added before cooking.

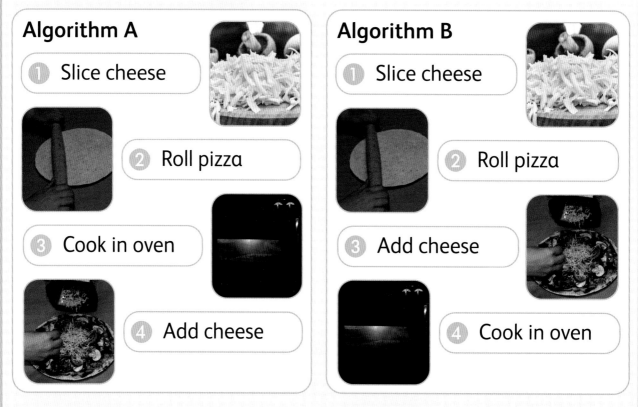

Algorithm A

1. Slice cheese
2. Roll pizza
3. Cook in oven
4. Add cheese

Algorithm B

1. Slice cheese
2. Roll pizza
3. Add cheese
4. Cook in oven

In Algorithm A, the cheese is not cooked!

Algorithm B is in the right order.
Algorithm A is not in the right order.

Practise

Look at the steps to make a fruit drink.

The steps are in the wrong order. Put the steps in the right order.

(A) Add fruit to blender

(B) Blend for 2 minutes

(C) Put the lid on blender

(D) Pour into a glass

(E) Add milk to blender

Finding errors in programs

Learn

Programs can also have errors.

Programs with errors may not work.

Errors in programs are called bugs.

Program for sunset

Here is the algorithm for a sunset.

Step	Instruction	
1	Start on Green Flag	🚩
2	Move 3 steps down	**3** ⬇
3	Hide sun	☀
4	Stop program	STOP

> **Keyword**
> **bug:** an error in a computer program

This ScratchJr code should match the algorithm. The code does not give the right result.

What is the error in the code?

The error in this program is in the first block.

The **Start on Tap** block is used instead of **Start on Green Flag**.

The correct program is:

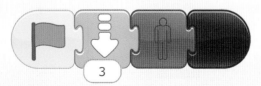

Practise

Program for driving a car

We want a car to move 5 steps right.
Open ScratchJr.

1   Find a Background with a road.
2   Select a **Driver** character.
3   Add this code to the **Driver** character.

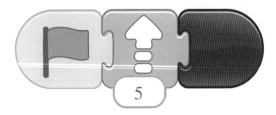

4   Run the program. What happens?

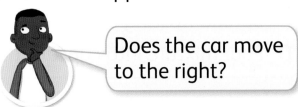

Does the car move
to the right?

Did you notice the error?
The error is the second block.
It should be a **Move Right** block as shown.

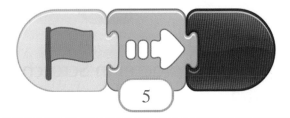

Go further

David is baking a cake.

1   Here is the algorithm.

Step	Instruction
1	Add ingredients to a bowl
2	Mix well
3	Bake in oven
4	Pour mixture into a pan

What is the error in this algorithm?

Computational thinking

David decides to make cupcakes instead.
What is the correct order of instructions?

STEP 1: A	A Mix ingredients
STEP 2: ?	B Bake in oven
STEP 3: ?	C Spread frosting on cupcakes
STEP 4: ?	D Pour mixture into cupcake tins

2   We want a dog to walk 5 steps right.
    Is this code correct?

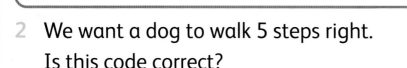

3   Add this code to a **Dog** character in ScratchJr.
    Do you get an error?

⭐ Challenge yourself!

Look at this algorithm for the **Dog** character to get to the **Cake** character.

Step	Instruction	
①	Start on Tap	👆
②	Move 3 steps left	**3** ⬅
③	Move 2 steps up	**2** ⬆
④	Move 5 steps left	**5** ⬅
⑤	Stop program	🛑 STOP

1   The code below does not match the algorithm.
    It has two errors. Circle the blocks with errors.

2   The code below is for the **Cake**.

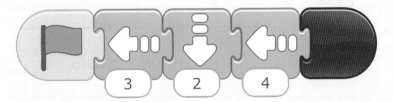

    What do you think the **Cake** will do?

3   Add the code to a **Cake** character in ScratchJr. What does the
    cake do?

My project

Amy is looking for tomatoes.

Here is the path to the tomatoes.

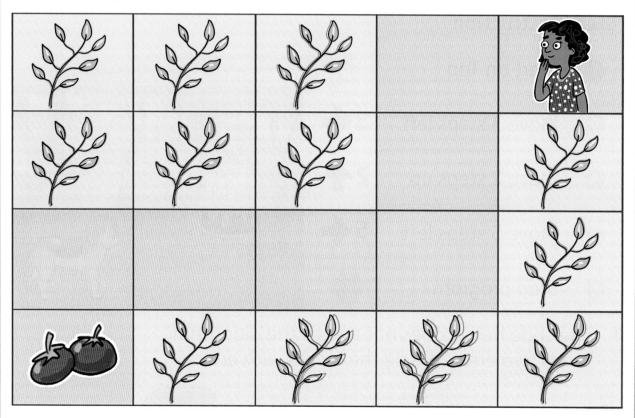

1   The algorithm has errors. Find the two errors.

Step	Instruction	
❶	Move 1 step left	**1 ⬅**
❷	Move 3 steps down	**3 ⬇**
❸	Move 1 step down	**1 ⬇**
❹	Move 3 steps left	**3 ⬅**

Now you will create a program. The program has a **Person** and an **Apple**. Here are the algorithms:

Step	Instruction	
❶	Start on Green Flag	🏳
❷	Move 15 steps left	**15**⬅
❸	Stop program	STOP

Step	Instruction	
❶	Start on Green Flag	🏳
❷	Wait for 30	⏱
❸	Shrink by 4	✳
❹	Stop program	STOP

2   Look at the code for the **Person** and the **Apple**.
There is an error in the code. Find the error and correct it.
Run your program with the correct code.

Did you know?

Errors in programs are called bugs. This is because a real bug got into a computer. It caused an error.

What can you do?

Read and review what you can do.
✔ I can find errors in algorithms.
✔ I can put instructions in the right order.
✔ I can find errors in programs.

Good job! Now you understand errors in algorithms and programs.

Computers in devices

Get started!

In a small group:

1 Name the devices in the pictures below.
2 What do these devices do? For example, the refrigerator keeps items cold.
3 Are any of the devices computers?

You will learn:

- that computers output information
- about everyday devices that use computers
- about robots.

In this unit, you will be able to describe various types of computers.

Warm up

Match the sentences below to the pictures.

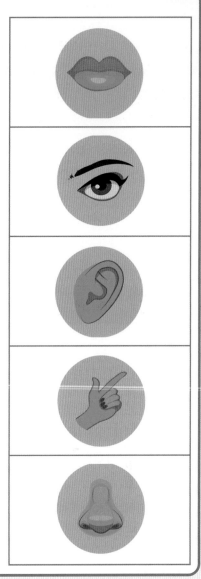

What can you hear with?	
What can you see with?	
What can you touch with?	
What can you smell with?	
What can you make sounds with?	

Do you remember?

Before starting this unit, check that you:
- remember that there are desktops, laptops, tablets and smartphones
- know that computers can run different programs
- know that data and information can be input into computers.

Output devices

Learn

Output devices connect to computers. Output devices allow you to see, hear or feel information.

Keywords

output: information that we can see, hear or feel

text: actual words that are written

Speakers and headphones let us hear sounds.

A screen for a computer is called a monitor.

A monitor lets us see videos, pictures and words.

Printers let us see text or pictures on paper.

Practise

Discuss in pairs.

1   What device can you use to read a letter?

2   What device can you use to print a picture?

3   What devices can you use to listen to music?

Computers control our devices

Learn

Lots of everyday devices use computers.

The computers are inside them.

The computers control the devices.

Keyword
control: in charge of

A refrigerator's computer keeps food cold.

A microwave's computer controls the cooking time.

In an air conditioner (AC), a computer keeps the room cool.

A washing machine's computer tells it how long to wash clothes.

Practise

Discuss with your partner:

Annay is trying to name devices that have a computer.

Can you help Annay?

1 Say the name of each device.

2 Say if you think the device has a computer inside it.

3 Say what the computer controls.

Did you know?

Some toys have computers inside them.

This toy dog barks when you push a button.

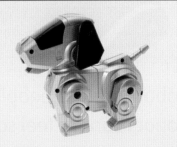

Robots can work

Keyword
robot: a machine that can do things without the help of a person

Learn

A robot is a machine that can do tasks without help.

A robot has a computer inside it. The computer controls the robot. Some robots look like people.

But some robots look different to people. It depends on the tasks that they are created to do.

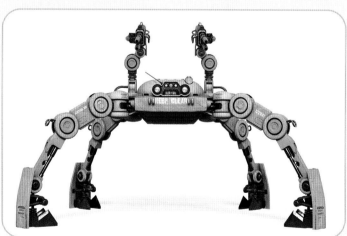

Robots are not people.
Robots cannot feel sad or happy.

Robots can be found in factories.

This is a robot that is used to build a car.

Robots can do work that is not safe for people.

This robot can touch things that would harm people.

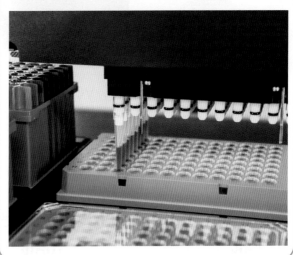

Robots can go to places that people cannot go.

This robot is on Mars.

Did you know?

Robots that look like humans are called androids.

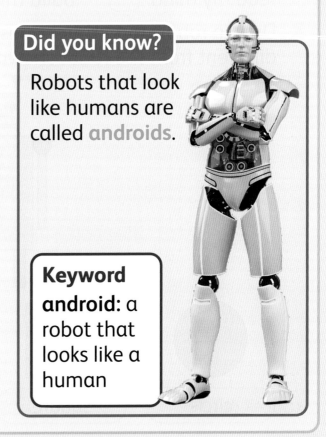

Keyword android: a robot that looks like a human

Practise

1   Are these robots? Circle yes or no.

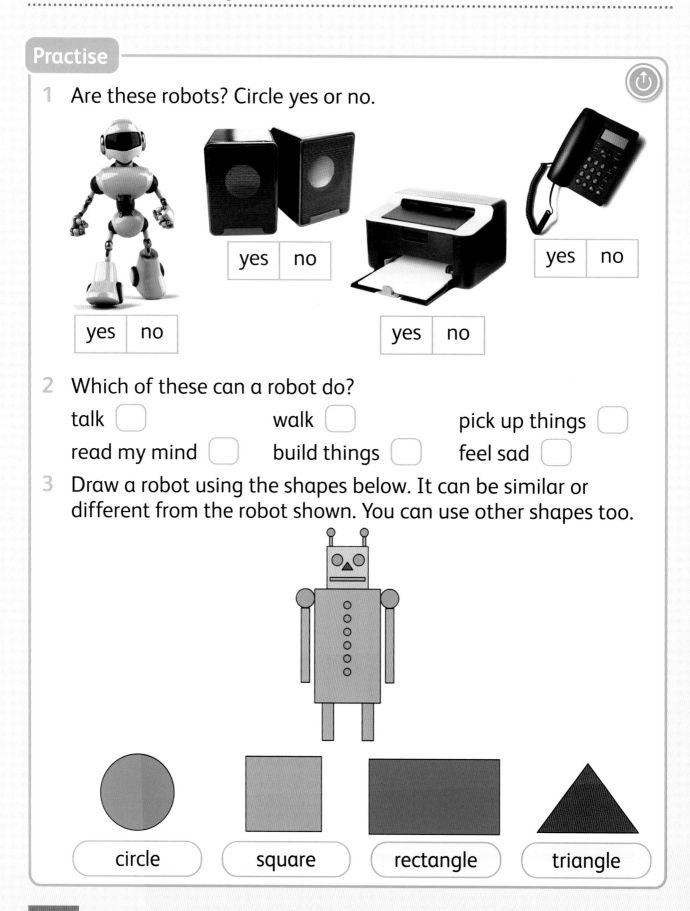

| yes | no |

| yes | no |

| yes | no |

| yes | no |

2   Which of these can a robot do?

talk ☐   walk ☐   pick up things ☐

read my mind ☐   build things ☐   feel sad ☐

3   Draw a robot using the shapes below. It can be similar or different from the robot shown. You can use other shapes too.

| circle | square | rectangle | triangle |

Go further

Hi, I'm Jack.

My friends have sent me some information.

Maris sang a song and sent it to me.

David wrote a letter.

Senya sent me some pictures of robots.

1   Point to the devices Jack can use to hear the song.
2   Point to the devices Jack can use to read the letter.
3   Point to the pictures of robots.

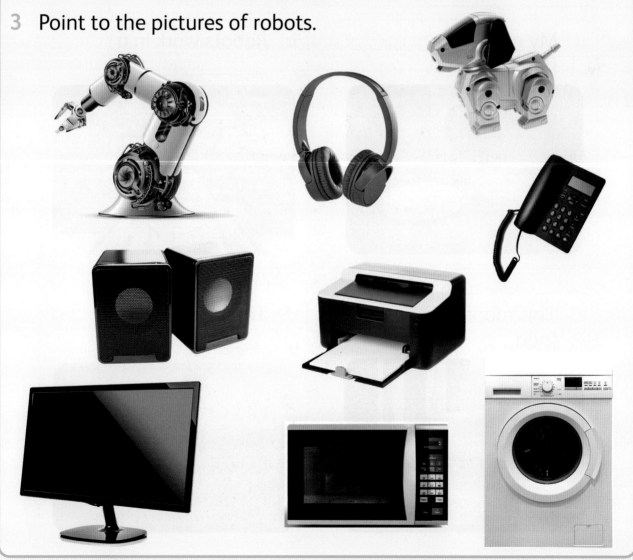

David said there is a computer in his washing machine.

4   Point to two other devices that have a computer.

5   Copy the sentences below. Use the correct word from the word bank to fill in the sentences.

(draw)   (sing)   (clean)   (factory)   (Mars)   (food)

(delivers)   (eats)

a   My robot can _____ floors.

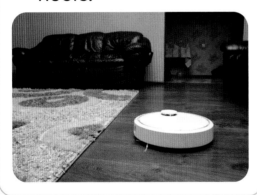

b   Robots work in a _____.

c   This robot _____ food.

d   This robot is on _____.

Challenge yourself!

1 Which devices have a computer inside them?

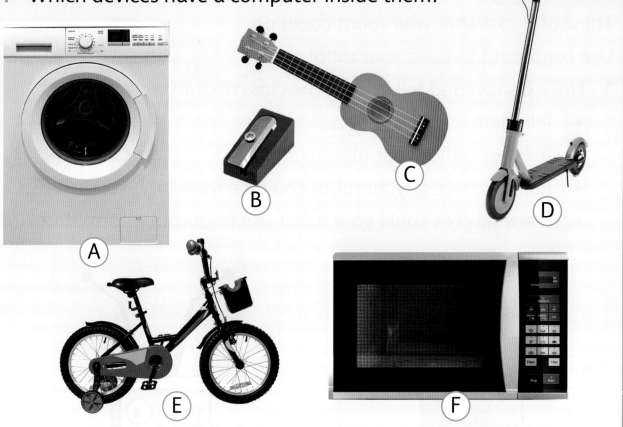

2 Say the name of this output device.

3 Say the name of this output device.

My project

You are going to design a new robot.

Think of a task that your robot could do.

Use cardboard to build your robot.

1 Have a show and tell. Talk to the class about your robot.

- Tell them what a robot is.
- Tell them what your robot can do.
- Tell them where your robot could be found.
- What devices could your robot use to output information?

Some toys have computers inside them.

2 Which of these toys do you think have computers in them?

☐ has computer
☐ does not have computer

☐ has computer
☐ does not have computer

☐ has computer
☐ does not have computer

☐ has computer
☐ does not have computer

☐ has computer
☐ does not have computer

What can you do?

Read and review what you can do.

✔ I know that computers output information.

✔ I know that some everyday devices use computers.

✔ I know what a robot is.

Well done! You now know about robots, and output devices.

Be a data collector

Recording data

Get started!

The pictures show people writing things. This has changed over time.

Discuss with a partner.
For each picture:

1 What is used to write things?
2 Point to the pictures that show how we write things today.

In this unit, you will learn about recording data and asking questions.

Stone Age – past

Technology Age – present

You will learn:

• about recording data
• about answering questions using data.

Warm up

Work in pairs.

1 Look at the **pictogram**.

   a How many people are sad?

   b How many people are happy?

   c How many people are mad?

Sad	😢 😢 😢
Happy	😊 😊 😊 😊 😊
Mad	😠 😠

2 Use the pictogram to complete the **table**.

   Count the emojis and write the number in the table.

   The first one is done for you.

   a How many people are sad?

   b How many people are happy?

   c How many people are mad?

3 Look at the pictogram and the table. What is the same? What is different?

Feelings	Number of people
Sad	3
Happy	
Mad	

Do you remember?

Before starting this unit, check that you:

• know that computing devices can answer questions

• know that computing devices can sort and organise data.

Recording data
Paper-based and electronic forms

Learn

Data can be recorded using a form.

Forms have a list of headings or questions.

People add details next to each heading or question.

> **Keyword**
> **record:** to collect

For instance, in this paper-based form, people can add:

- their name and age
- their favourite colour
- their favourite movie.

ALL ABOUT ME

NAME: _____ AGE: _____

FAVOURITE THING TO DO: _____

FAVOURITE COLOUR: _____

FAVOURITE MOVIE: _____

FAVOURITE FOOD: _____

Data can be collected on a paper-based form. This data is then entered into a computer.

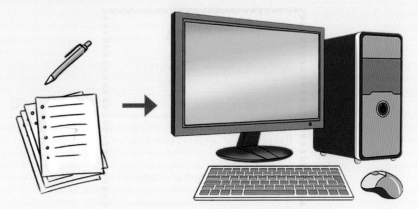

An electronic form is displayed on a computer screen.

The keyboard and mouse are used to enter data onto the form.

- The keyboard is used to type letters and numbers.
- The mouse is used to click an option.

Personal data entry form	
Enter personal data details	
Required fields are represented by (*)	
Registration number:	_____ (*)
Password:	_____ (*)
Last name:	_____ (*)
First name:	_____ (*)
Middle name:	_____ (*)
Marital status:	MARRIED ⌄ (*)

Data collected using electronic forms is stored in a computer. This is faster than copying data from a paper-based form into a computer.

Keyword
electronic: on a computer

Practise

1   The picture shows a paper-based form.

> ## Pet form
>
> Pet's name: [Scruffy]
>
> Type of animal: [dog]
>
> Reason for visit: [checkup]
>
> Heartbeat: good ☑ bad ☐
>
> Temperature: [37°C]
>
> Shots: yes ☐   no ☑

Discuss with a partner. What device (keyboard or mouse) will be used to enter the following data? Tick (✔) the answer for each:

		Keyboard	Mouse
A	Pet's name		
B	Type of animal		
C	Reason for visit		
D	Heartbeat: good or bad		
E	Temperature		
F	Shots: yes or no		

2   Tell your partner which picture shows the faster way to enter data into the computer. Explain your choice to your partner.

OR

Recording data
Using Google Forms

> **Keywords**
> **online:** connected to the internet
> **link:** something you click on

Learn

Google Forms is a type of electronic form.

Google Forms is an online form.

To fill out Google Forms, you need:

1 a device – for example, a computer
2 internet access
3 a link to Google Forms.

Google Forms can have different types of questions.

- A keyboard is used to type the answers to short answer questions.
- A mouse is used to select checkboxes.

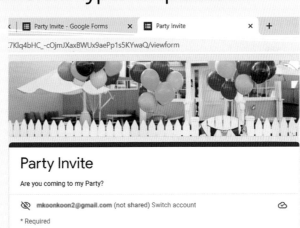

Party Invite - Google Forms ✕   Party Invite ✕ +

7Klq4bHC_-cOjmJXaxBWUx9aePp1s5KYwaQ/viewform

Party Invite

Are you coming to my Party?

mkoonkoon2@gmail.com (not shared) Switch account

* Required

What is your name?

Your answer

Can you attend? *

◯ Yes, I'll be there

◯ Sorry, can't make it

Submit   Clear form

> Type using the keyboard

> Click to select the option using the mouse

Here is an example of Google Forms.

Practise

You will need a computer for this activity.

Your teacher has created a Google Forms template called 'About me'.

Follow these steps:

1   Click on the link that is shared with you. The form should open.
2   Answer the questions on the form.
3   Click the 'Submit' button when you are done.

About Me

Form description

What is your name?   *

Short answer text

Do you have a pet?

○ YES

○ NO

What is your favourite colour?

○ Red

○ Blue

○ Yellow

○ Green

○ Other...

You cannot use Google Forms if you do not have internet access.

Recording data
Using data tables

Learn

Grouping data makes it easier to understand.
A **data table** can be used to group data.

Table 1

Name	Sport
John	Swimming
Mary	Tennis
Danny	Soccer
Ted	Swimming
Tom	Soccer
Sally	Soccer
Adam	Soccer
Ria	Swimming

Table 1 shows some children's favourite sports:

- Swimming
- Tennis
- Soccer

Table 2 groups this data.
It shows the number of students who like each sport.

Table 2

Sport	Number of students	
Swimming	3	
Tennis	1	
Soccer	4	

Keyword

data table: a table that shows data

109

Look at this table.

Sport	Number of students	
Soccer	4	🧍🧍🧍🧍
Swimming	3	🧍🧍🧍
Tennis	1	🧍

The number of students is now in order.

We can use the table to ask questions like:

- How many students like swimming?
- Which is the least popular sport?

What other questions can you ask using the data table?

A group of data with things in common is called a category.

Practise

1 True or false?

   a A data table is used to group data.

   b Grouping data makes it hard to understand.

   c We can answer questions using a data table.

2 Work in pairs.
The data table shows favourite ice-creams.

   a How many ice-cream flavours are in the data table?

   b Say the names of the groups.

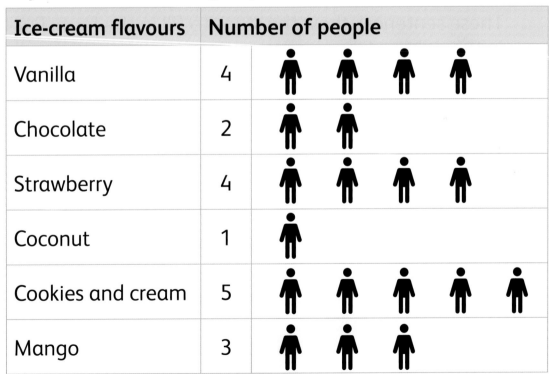

Ice-cream flavours	Number of people	
Vanilla	4	👤 👤 👤 👤
Chocolate	2	👤 👤
Strawberry	4	👤 👤 👤 👤
Coconut	1	👤
Cookies and cream	5	👤 👤 👤 👤 👤
Mango	3	👤 👤 👤

3 Which is the least popular ice-cream?

4 Which is the most popular ice-cream?

Go further

1 Mrs Smith is having a class party. She created a Google Forms template to collect some data from the class.

Class Party Form

Name of child _____

Are you coming to the party?
☐ yes   ☐ no   ☐ not sure

What are you bringing?
☐ food   ☐ snacks   ☐ drinks

---

a These sentences show the steps to fill in the form. Put them in the right order.

| A | Answer the questions on the form. |

| B | Click the 'Submit' button to submit answers. |

| C | Click the link to open the form. |

b Which device will you use to answer each question:

• keyboard

• or mouse?

2   Draw four lines to connect the words on the left to the
    correct sentences.

Data table	Used to collect data
Mouse	Shows data that is grouped
Form	A type of electronic form
Google Forms	Used to make a selection on a form

Data table

Name	Sport
John	Swimming
Mary	Tennis
Danny	Soccer

Mouse

Form

Pet form
Pet's name: Scruffy
Type of animal: dog
Reason for visit: checkup

Google Forms

Do you have a pet?
○ YES
○ NO

3   This data table shows some data that was collected by
    Mrs Smith.

    a   How many groups are in the data table?
    b   Write two questions that you can ask using the data shown
        in the table.

Items		Number of students	
Drinks		5	🧍 🧍 🧍 🧍 🧍
Food		5	🧍 🧍 🧍 🧍 🧍
Snacks		3	🧍 🧍 🧍

Challenge yourself!

1   Many people use forms to collect data.

For example, doctors use forms to collect data about their patients.

Draw a line to match the type of form with the data to be collected.

Type of form
School form
Pet form
Club form
Hospital form

Data to be collected
Type of animal
Name of club
Patient's name
Age of student

2   a   Point to the electronic form.

b   Point to the paper-based form.

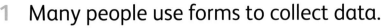

ALL ABOUT ME

NAME: _____ AGE: _____

FAVOURITE THING TO DO: _____

FAVOURITE COLOUR: _____

FAVOURITE MOVIE: _____

FAVOURITE FOOD: _____

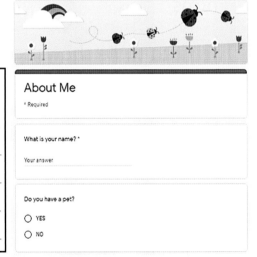

About Me

* Required

What is your name? *

Your answer

Do you have a pet?

○ YES

○ NO

3   The data table shows some how many children own each toy.

a   How many groups of toys are there?

b   Tell a partner three questions you can ask about the data in the table.

Toys	Number of children	
Dolls	7	👤👤👤👤👤👤👤
Cars	5	👤👤👤👤👤
Blocks	9	👤👤👤👤👤👤👤👤👤

My project

1   Jacob's class is going to a farm. Pretend you are going on the field trip. Complete the Google Forms template. Your teacher will share the link with you.

Field Trip to the Farm
Form description

Enter full name   *

Short answer text

Are you visiting the farm?

◯ Yes

◯ No

Will you be taking the school bus?

◯ Yes

◯ No

What are you bringing?

◯ Water

◯ Snacks

◯ Sandwiches

◯ Other...

Do you have any allergies?

◯ Yes

◯ No

Jacob created a form to collect data.

He needs to know how many animals each farmer has.

Discuss with a partner:

2 Which form might be better to collect data from the farmers:
   • a paper-based form?
   • an electronic form?
   Explain your choice.

3 Jacob collected data from the farmers.
   It is shown in this data table.

Animal	Farmer Joe	Farmer Sam
chickens	10	9
ducks	9	6
goats	7	5
sheep	6	6
rabbits	8	10
horses	6	8

   a How many groups of animals are in the data table?
   b Work with your partner. Think about questions that can be asked about the data shown in the table.
   Share your questions with the class.

Did you know?

Did you know that data was first recorded in the form of tally marks?

What can you do?

Read and review what you can do.

✔ I know you can record data using a form.

✔ I know you can answer questions using a data table.

Awesome! Now you know about forms and data tables.

Unit 9 Be a games developer

Creating computer games

Get started!

Work in groups of four. Do you like these types of computer games? What is your favourite?

① Action games

② Adventure games

③ Puzzle games

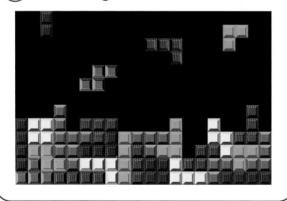

④ Sports games

You will learn:

- to run and test programs
- to find errors in programs
- about debugging.

In this unit, you will create computer games.

Warm up

Work in pairs.

What is the missing picture in each line?

Each line has a pattern that repeats.

     A

 or

       B

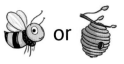
 or

      C

 or

Do you remember?

Before starting this unit, check that you:
- can put instructions in order
- can find errors in algorithms
- know how to create a program from an algorithm.

There is an online chapter all about ScratchJr.

Bugs in computer games
Testing programs

Learn

We need to check that programs work.
This is called testing a program.
We want a **Frog** to jump 2 steps, then jump 4 steps. Here is the algorithm and the code.

Step	Instruction	
1	Start on Tap	👆
2	Jump 2 steps	🧍
3	Jump 4 steps	🧍
4	Stop program	STOP

Keyword
testing: checking if a program works

Can you predict what happens?

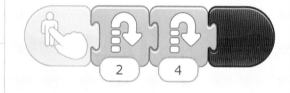

To test this program:
1 Select a Background.
2 Select a **Frog** character.
3 Add the blocks of code above.
4 Tap the **Frog** to test the code.

This program gives the right result. When we tap the **Frog**, it jumps 2 steps up and then 4 steps up.

Practise

1 Open the game from page 120.
2 Here is a new algorithm for the **Frog**. This is the new result we want in the game.

Step	Instruction	
①	Start on Tap	👆
②	Jump 8 grid squares	🧍
③	Say "Ribbit"	💬
④	Stop program	STOP

3 Here is the new code for the **Frog**:

4 Change your program to the new code for the **Frog**. Test this code.
5 We want to add a **Snake** to the game.
Here is the algorithm for the **Snake**.

Step	Instruction	
①	Start on Green Flag	🚩
②	Play Pop sound	POP
③	Move 6 steps right	**6**➡
④	Stop program	STOP

6 Select a **Snake** character.
7 Create the code to match the algorithm.
8 Test your program. Did you get the right result?

Finding errors

Learn

Sometimes a program does not give the right result. This means it has an error.

To find errors, we compare the algorithm to the program.

We will create a new game in ScratchJr with three characters.

The algorithm below is for the **Cat Walking** character.

Step	Instruction	
1	Start on Purple message	✉
2	Move 1 step right	1 ➡
3	Stop program	STOP

Here is the code for this algorithm. This program does not give the right result.

Can you predict what happens?

It has one error in the **Move Right** block.

Practise

Create the program for this game in ScratchJr.

1 Select a Background.

2 Select the **Cat Walking** character.

3 Add this code to the **Cat Walking** character.

4 Test the code by clicking the Purple message block.

5 What is the error in the **Move Right** block?

The second character is the **Soccer Ball**. This algorithm is for the **Soccer Ball**.

Step	Instruction	
❶	Start on Bump	🏃
❷	Move 2 steps right	2➡
❸	Stop program	🛑 STOP

Here is the code for this algorithm:

6 Add the **Soccer Ball** and the code.

7 Test your program. Did you get the right result? Find any errors.

You now have code for **2** out of **3** characters.

Debugging code

Keyword
debug: to find and correct an error in a program

Learn

If you find errors, you can correct them.

Correcting errors is called debugging.

We can debug the **Cat Walking** code.

In the algorithm on page 122, the **Cat Walking** moves 1 step right.

We can change 2 to 1 in the **Move Right** block. Now the code matches the algorithm.

We can also debug the **Soccer Ball** code.

There was an error in the **first** block.

The algorithm on page 123 began with **Start on Bump**. The code used a **Start on Tap** block.

We can correct this so that the code matches the algorithm.

Practise

1 Debug the **Cat Walking** and **Soccer Ball** code. Change the code as shown on page 124.

2 Add a **Star** character.

3 Here is the algorithm for the **Star**.

Step	Instruction	
❶	Start on Tap	👆
❷	Send Purple Start Message	✉️
❸	Stop program	STOP

4 Add this code to the **Star** character.

5 Test your program.

6 Debug your program to get the right result.

When you press the **Star**, the **Cat Walking** should move right.

When the **Cat Walking** touches the ball, the **Soccer Ball** should move.

Go further

You will create a new game. Here is an algorithm for a **Frog**:

Step	Instruction	
1	Start on Tap	👆
2	Turn right (5)	**5** ↱
3	Stop program	STOP

1 Open a new project.

2 Add a **Frog** character and this code. Does the code match the algorithm?

3 Run the program.
   Here is an algorithm for a **Snake**.

Step	Instruction	
1	Start on Tap	👆
2	Grow (by 2)	**2** ✳
3	Move 5 steps left	**5** ⬅
4	Stop program	STOP

4 Add a **Snake** character and this code to your program.

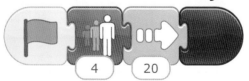

5 Test the code.
6 Does the program give the right result?
7 Debug your code.

Challenge yourself!

Using your game from the last page:

1 Add the **Bat** character.

Adventure game

2 Add code to the **Bat**.
The code should match this algorithm.

Step	Instruction	
1	Start on Green Message	✉
2	Move 1 step up	1⬆
3	Stop program	STOP

3 Draw a **Green Button** using the **Paint Editor**.

4 Add code to the **Green Button** to match this algorithm:

Step	Instruction	
1	Start on Tap	👆
2	Send Green Start Message	✉
3	Stop program	STOP

The **Green Button** controls the **Frog**.

5 Test your program. Does it give the right result?

6 If not, check for errors and correct them.

My project

You will create an **Action Game** in ScratchJr.

1 Create a new project and add the **Space** background.
2 Look at the algorithm and code for the **Rocket**.

Step	Instruction	
①	Start on Tap	👆
②	Set speed to fast	
③	Move 15 steps up	**15** ⬆
④	Stop program	STOP

3 Add the **Rocket** and code.
4 Test your program. Does it match the algorithm?
5 Look at the algorithm and code for a **Planet** character.

Step	Instruction	
①	Start on Bump	🏃🚶
②	Play pop sound	POP
③	Hide character	🧍
④	Stop program	STOP

6 Add the **Planet** and code.
7 Test your program.
8 Debug your code.

The **Planet** cannot be seen if the **Rocket** hits it.

Did you know?

- One of the earliest computer games was called Pong.
- It was like a game of table tennis.
- It looks different to modern games!

What can you do?

Read and review what you can do.

✔ I can run and test programs.
✔ I can find errors in programs.
✔ I know about debugging.

Great, now you can create and debug programs!

Unit 10 We are connected

Networks with and without wires

Get started!

Work with your partner:

- Get two paper cups, a length of string, two paper clips and a pencil.
- Pass the string through a hole in each cup.
- Pull the string tight. Ask your partner to speak into one cup. You listen through the other.

Did you hear what your partner said?
How do you think it happened?

You will learn:

- that some devices connect to a network with wires
- that some devices connect to a network without wires
- that sometimes a device has no internet access.

In this unit, you will learn about networks connected with and without wires.

Warm up

Discuss with your partner the differences between the two phones in the picture.

1 Which phone allows you to talk while moving?

2 Why do you think you can move with this phone?

3 Which phone do you prefer?

4 Tell your partner why you prefer the phone you chose.

Do you remember?

Before starting this unit, check that you:

- know that some devices can connect to a network
- know that the internet is made of lots of computers connected around the world.

Networks
Network with wires

Learn

Two or more computers can connect together.

When computers connect together, it is called a network.

Some devices can also connect to a network.

Computers connected to a network can:

- talk to each other
- share devices
- share data.

Computers and devices can connect to a network with wires.

Some common examples are:

- printers
- desktop computers
- games consoles.

Can you think of other devices that connect to a network with a wire?

Keyword
wire: tubes that let data move between devices

Practise

1   Say each word and point to the picture.

(printer)   (tablet)   (camera)   (smartphone)

2   Choose the devices below that commonly connect to a network with a wire.

3   Choose the correct word to complete the sentence.

(rope)   (strings)   (wires)   (ribbons)

Devices can connect to a network using _____.

4   Choose the correct words to complete the sentence.

(books)   (pencils)   (printers)

Devices connected to a network with a wire can share

_____.

Networks
Networks without wires

Some devices can connect to a network without wires.

You can use a smartphone, laptop or tablet when you are in a park, on a train or bus.

This is possible because they can connect to a network without wires.

At home you can send a letter from your smartphone to your printer.

This is possible because both devices can connect to a network without wires.

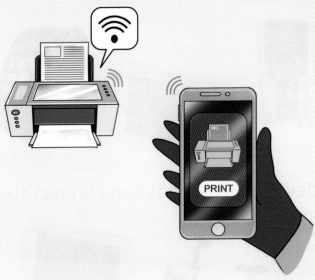

Here are some devices that can connect to a network without wires:

Laptops

Games console

Smartwatches

Tablets

Cameras

Smartphones

Smart glasses

Can you think of any other devices that can connect to a network without wires?

Which devices can connect with or without wires?

Practise

1   Say each word and point to the correct picture.

(tablet)   (desktop)   (games console)   (smartwatch)

2   Choose the devices below that can connect to a network without a wire.

3   Say if the following statements are true or false.

		True	False
a	All devices use wires to connect to a network.		
b	Some devices connect to a network without wires.		
c	A scooter connects to a network without a wire.		
d	A smartphone connects to a network without a wire.		
e	A camera connects to a network with a wire.		

Internet access
Are you connected?

Learn

Sometimes messages will not send.

Sometimes online videos will not play.

If a video will not play, you will see the 'circle loading' animation.

> **Keyword**
> **animation:** moving images

Sometimes a message also appears saying 'No internet' or 'Connect to the internet'.

These messages mean the internet is not available on your device.

Without internet access you cannot:

watch your favourite online videos 	listen to your favourite online songs 
video call your friends 	send or receive emails 
share pictures 	find information on the World Wide Web 

Did you know?

Without internet access, you can still do things offline.

For example, you can:
- read emails stored on your computer
- view pictures stored on your computer
- listen to music stored on your computer
- view videos stored on your computer.

Keyword
offline: not connected to the internet

Practise

1   Your device is not connected to the internet.
    Tick (✔) the things you can do.

    a   ◯ Look up things on the internet

    b   ◯ Video chat with friends

    c   ◯ Draw a picture

    d   ◯ Play online games

2   Look at the following picture.

When could this picture appear on your device? There are two
possible answers. Talk with your partner.

    a   Because my device is connected to the internet
    b   Because my online video is not working
    c   Because the internet is not available on my device
    d   Because my device is not working

Go further

Say if the following statements are true or false.

a A laptop can connect to a network without a wire.

b A tablet can connect to a network with a wire.

c A camera can share pictures with computers connected to the network.

d I can share photos if my device is connected to the internet.

e The internet is always available.

f I can play online games if my device is connected to the internet.

Challenge yourself!

1 Can a smartwatch connect to a network with a wire? Discuss the answer with your partner.

Can you think of any reasons for your answer?

2 Name three devices that can connect to a network with wires.

3 Name three devices that can connect to a network without wires.

My project

Draw two computers and a printer connected with a wire.

Draw another picture to show any three devices connected without wires.

Tell your partner why you chose these three devices.

What can you do?

Read and review what you can do.

✔ I can name devices that connect to a network with wires.

✔ I can name devices that can connect to a network without wires.

✔ I know that sometimes there is no internet access.

Great work! You now know more about networks and the internet.

Creating shapes

Get started!

In groups of four:
- Talk about what you like to draw.
- Say which shapes you can draw.
- Choose one shape. Show how to draw it.

You will learn:
- to give directions (forward, backward, left, right)
- to give instructions for a simple task.

In this unit, you will write instructions and draw shapes.

Warm up

Work in pairs. Draw the shapes below:

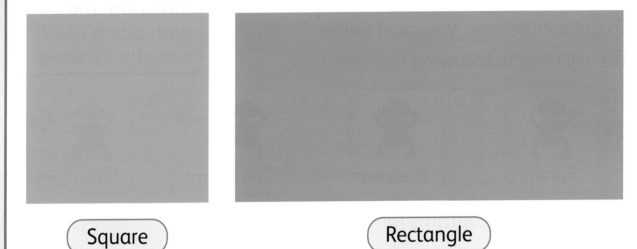

Square

Rectangle

1 How many sides does each shape have?
2 How many corners does each shape have?
3 Which shape has sides with equal length?
4 Show the steps you took to draw each shape.

Do you remember?

Before starting this unit, check that you:
• know that an algorithm is a set of instructions
• know the order of instructions is important.

Giving directions

Keyword
direction: the path along which something moves

To get somewhere, you must follow directions. We will use the following four directions:

| 1 Forward | 2 Backward | 3 Turn Right | 4 Turn Left |

We will write algorithms for each direction.

A robot can move forward or backward by a set distance.

The algorithm to move forward by a step is:

Step	Instruction	
①	Start program	🚩
②	(Move forward 1 step)	
③	Stop program	STOP

The algorithm to move backward by a step is:

Step	Instruction	
①	Start program	🚩
②	(Move backward 1 step)	
③	Stop program	STOP

The algorithm to turn right is:

Step	Instruction	
1	Start program	🚩
2	(Turn right)	
3	Stop program	STOP

The algorithm to turn left is:

Step	Instruction	
1	Start program	🚩
2	(Turn left)	
3	Stop program	STOP

Moving through a path

1   Here is the algorithm to move along the path shown:

Step	Instruction	
1	Start program	🚩
2	Move forward 1 step	
3	Turn left	
4	Move forward 1 step	
5	Stop program	STOP

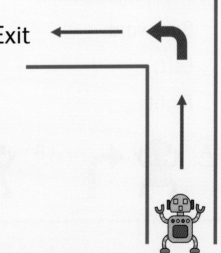

Exit

2 The path has changed. Here is the algorithm to move along this path:

Step	Instruction	
①	Start program	⚑
②	Move forward 1 step	🤖↑
③	Turn left	🤖↰
④	Move forward 1 step	🤖↑
⑤	Move forward 1 step	🤖↑
⑥	Stop program	STOP

Exit ← ← ↰

Practise

1 Match each direction with the arrows:

Forward: ___

Backward: ___

Left: ___

Right: ___

 (A)   (B)   (C)    (D)

Practise

2   The algorithm below is for this maze. It is in the wrong order.
    Put the steps in the right order for the robot to reach the exit.
    The first two are done for you.

F, A, ___, ___, ___, ___, ___, G

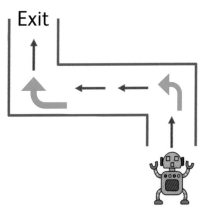

Step	Instruction	
A	Move forward 1 step	
B	Move forward 1 step	
C	Turn right	
D	Move forward 1 step	
E	Turn left	
F	Start program	
G	Stop program	
H	Move forward 1 step	

Drawing shapes

Algorithm to draw two lines of a square

Look at the steps to draw a square.

Step ① Move a step forward

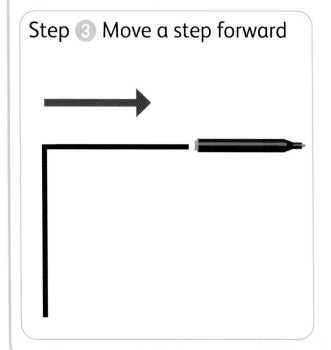

Step ② Turn right

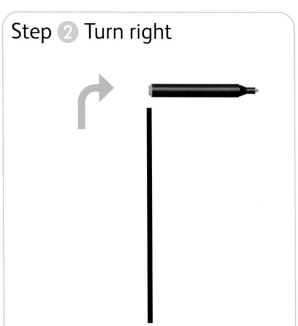

Step ③ Move a step forward

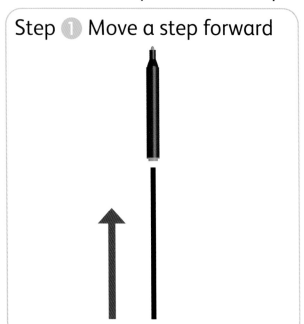

Step ④ Turn right

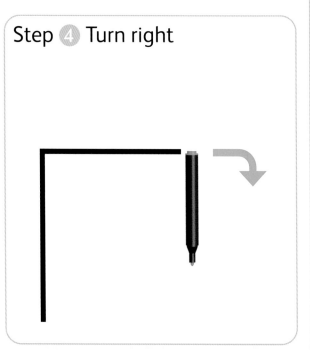

Practise

1   Work in pairs. Put the steps in the right order to finish
    drawing a square. The first four steps were completed
    in the **Learn** panel.

Step __: Move a step forward

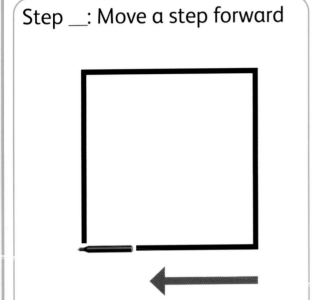

Step __: Turn right

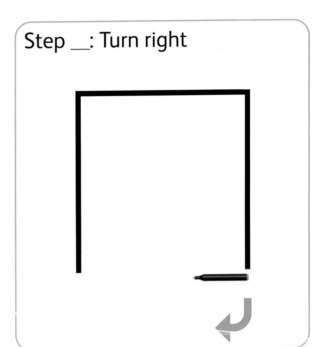

Step __: Turn right

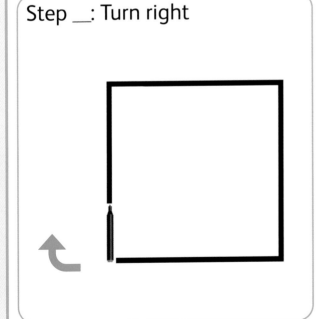

Step __: Move a step forward

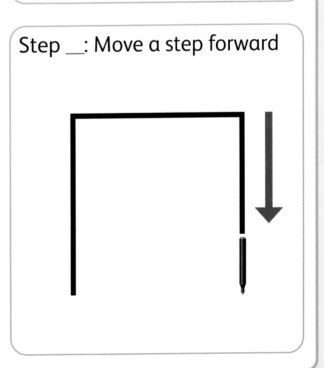

Go further

Computational thinking

1   See the steps below to draw two lines of a rectangle.
    Circle the correct answer in each step.
    Steps 1, 2 and 3 are completed for you.

Step ❶

(Start)/ **Stop** program

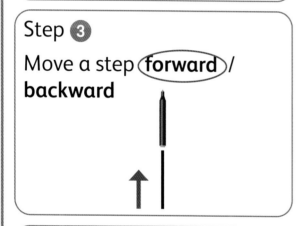

Step ❷

Put the pen **up** /(down)

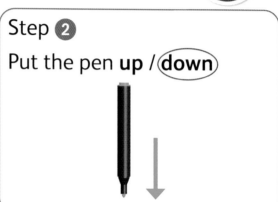

Step ❸

Move a step (forward)/ **backward**

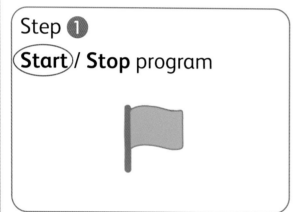

Step ❹

Turn **left / right**

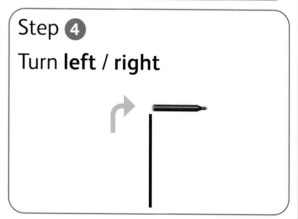

Step ❺

Move a step **forward / backward**

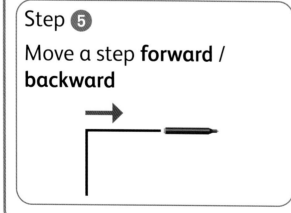

Step ❻

Move a step **forward / backward**

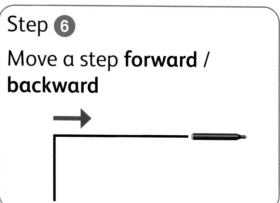

Step **7**

Turn **left / right**

2   Work in pairs with pencil and paper.

Use the algorithm on page 150.

Follow the steps to draw the two lines of a rectangle.

3   The algorithm below is for this maze.

a   Test this algorithm.
Does it follow the
path through
the maze?

b   Which step has an error?

c   Write your own algorithm.
Check with your partner.
Does it get you to
the end?

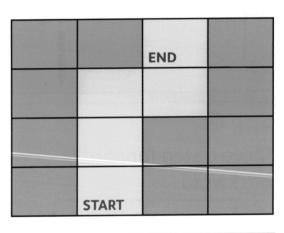

Step	Instruction	
A	Move forward 1 step	
B	Move forward 1 step	
C	Turn right	
D	Move forward 1 step	
E	Turn right	
F	Move forward 1 step	

Challenge yourself!

Computational thinking

1   Complete the algorithm for the rectangle.
    Circle the correct answer in each step.

Step ⑧

Move a step **forward** /
backward

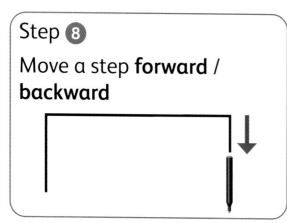

Step ⑨

Turn **left** / **right**

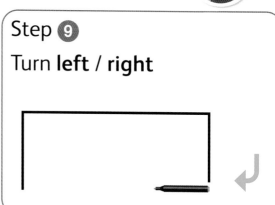

Step ⑩

Move a step **forward** /
backward

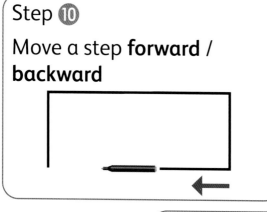

Step ⑪

Move a step **backward** /
forward

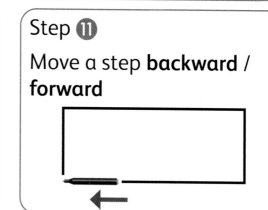

Step ⑫

Turn **left** / **right**

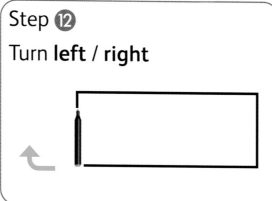

2   Work in pairs with pencil and paper.
    Use the algorithm on page 152.
    Follow the steps to draw the rest of the rectangle.

3   The algorithm below is for this maze.

    a   Test this algorithm.
        Does it follow the path
        through the maze?

    b   Which step has an error?

    c   Write your own
        algorithm. Check with
        your partner. Does it
        get you to the end?

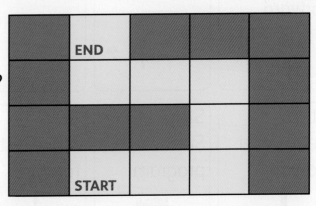

Step	Instruction	
A	Turn right	
B	Move forward 1 step	
C	Move forward 1 step	
D	Turn left	
E	Move forward 1 step	
F	Move forward 1 step	
G	Turn left	
H	Move forward 1 step	
I	Move forward 1 step	
J	Move forward 1 step	

My project

1   This is a different way to draw a square. Put the steps in the correct order.

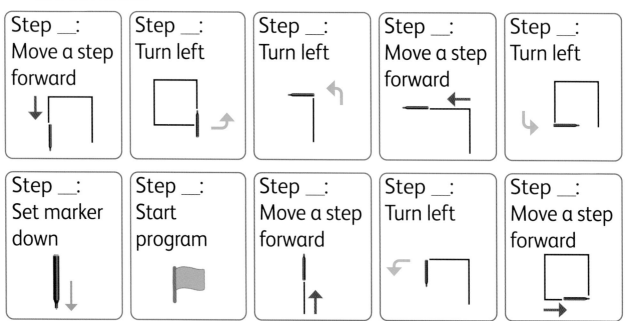

Step __:
Move a step forward

Step __:
Turn left

Step __:
Turn left

Step __:
Move a step forward

Step __:
Turn left

Step __:
Set marker down

Step __:
Start program

Step __:
Move a step forward

Step __:
Turn left

Step __:
Move a step forward

2   Work in pairs with pencil and paper. Use the algorithm to draw the square.

3   We can draw the number '8' using two squares. To do this we add more steps to the algorithm in question 1.
   a   First we need to replace step 10. A new step 10 is shown below.
   b   Put the rest of the extra steps in the right order. You need to add steps 11 to 15.
   c   Work in pairs with a new piece of paper. Follow steps 1–15 to draw the number '8'.

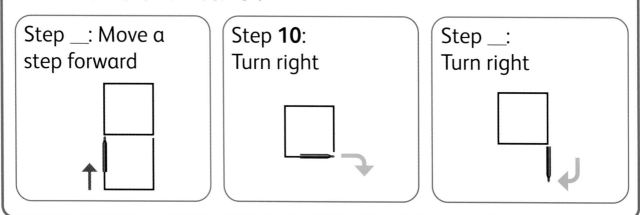

Step __: Move a step forward

Step **10:**
Turn right

Step __:
Turn right

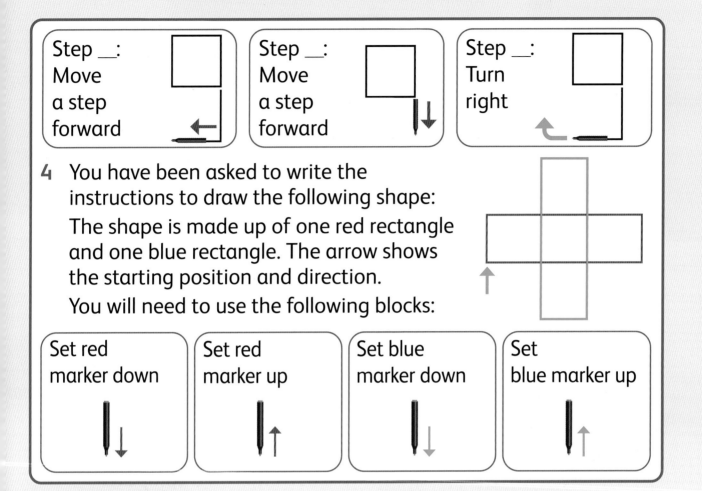

Step __:
Move a step forward

Step __:
Move a step forward

Step __:
Turn right

4   You have been asked to write the instructions to draw the following shape:

The shape is made up of one red rectangle and one blue rectangle. The arrow shows the starting position and direction.

You will need to use the following blocks:

Set red marker down

Set red marker up

Set blue marker down

Set blue marker up

Did you know?

There are shapes all around us:

What can you do?

Read and review what you can do.

✔ I can give directions (forward, backward, left, right).

✔ I can give instructions for a simple task.

Great job! Now you know how to give instructions!

Glossary

A

algorithm: a set of instructions for a task or problem

android: a robot that looks like a human

animation: moving images

app: this is another name for a program

B

bug: an error in a computer program

C

category: a group of data that has something in common

code: commands that tell a computer what to do

communicate: share information, news, or ideas

computing device: a machine that works with data

control: in charge of

D

data: numbers, words, pictures, sounds or videos

data table: a table that shows data

debug: to find and correct an error in a program

device: printers, mice and keyboards are all examples of devices

direction: the path along which something moves

Turn Right

E

electronic: on a computer

error: a mistake in an algorithm or program

I

instructions: information about how something should be done

L

link: something you click on

N

network: two or more computers connected together

O

offline: not connected to the internet

online: connected to the internet

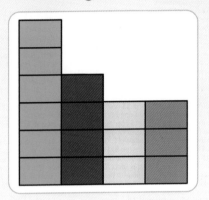

organise: to arrange items or data in some order

outcome: result

output: information that we can see or hear or feel

P

program: a set of code that completes a task

program or **software:** a set of instructions for the computer to follow

R

record: to collect

robot: a machine that can do certain things without the help of a person

S

sort: to group items or data that have something in common

T

task: an activity

testing: to check if a program works

text: actual words that are written

W

wire: tubes that let data move between devices

Acknowledgements

The Publishers would like to thank the following for permission to reproduce copyright material. Every effort has been made to trace or contact all copyright holders, but if any have been inadvertently overlooked, the Publishers will be pleased to make the necessary arrangements at the first opportunity.

Text acknowledgements
pp. 4–7, 17, 20, 24, 30–34, 48–63, 76–79, 82–87, 119–129 © Scratch is developed by the Lifelong Kindergarten Group at the MIT Media Lab. See http://scratch.mit.edu. Licensed under a Creative Commons Attribution-ShareAlike 2.0 Generic license (CC BY-SA 2.0); **p. 17** © Google Classroom is a trademark of Google LLC. Google and Google Docs are trademarks of Google LLC and this book is not endorsed by or affiliated with Google in any way; **pp. 17, 20** Mojang © 2009-2022. "Minecraft" is a trademark of Mojang AB; **pp. 17, 20** © Used with permission from Microsoft; **pp. 107–108, 112–113, 115** © Google Forms is a trademark of Google LLC. Google and Google Docs are trademarks of Google LLC and this book is not endorsed by or affiliated with Google in any way.

Photo acknowledgements
p. 4 cl, p. 49 tl © Jiaking 1/Adobe Stock Photo; p. 4 cc, p. 49 tc © Jiaking 1/Adobe Stock Photo; p. 4 cc, p. 49 tc © Jiaking 1/Adobe Stock Photo; p. 4 cc, p. 49 cr © Jiaking 1/Adobe Stock Photo; p. 5 –7, p. 17 cc, p. 20 cl, p. 30–34, p. 50–62, p. 78–79, p. 82–85, p. 87, p. 120–129, p. 157 © Scratch is developed by the Lifelong Kindergarten Group at the MIT Media Lab. See http://scratch.mit.edu. Licensed under a Creative Commons Attribution-ShareAlike 2.0 Generic license (CC BY-SA 2.0); p. 7 cl, p. 70bl © Stockphoto-Graf/Adobe Stock Photo; p. 10 tr © Yakobchuk Olena/Adobe Stock Photo; p. 10 cr © Rafael Ramirez/Adobe Stock Photo; p. 10 cb, p. 12 tr, p. 68 cr, p. 71 cc, p. 99 bc, p. 133 cc, p. 141 cc, p. 156 tr © Maxim Kazmin/Adobe Stock Photo; p. 11 tc, p. 68 cl, p. 69 cl, p. 71 tc, p. 136 cr © Graphics RF/Adobe Stock Photo; p. 11 cr, p. 133 cc, p. 135 cl, p. 136 cc © Time 4 Studio/Adobe Stock Photo; p. 11 cr, p. 13 cr © Frog/Adobe Stock Photo; p. 12 tl © Destina/Adobe Stock Photo; p. 12 tc, p. 46 tl © WDnet Studio/Adobe Stock Photo; p. 12 tc, p. 46 cc © Frog/Adobe Stock Photo; p. 12 cl, p. 90 cc, p. 91 tc, cc, p. 96 tc, p. 97 cl, p. 99 cc © Lamaip/Adobe Stock Photo; p. 12 cc © Billion Photos.com/Adobe Stock Photo; p. 12 cr © Scanrail/Adobe Stock Photo; p. 12 cc, p. 69 tr, p. 136 c © Maxim Kazmin/Adobe Stock Photo; p. 12 cc, p. 141 cr © Nurbek/Adobe Stock Photo; p. 12 bl © Gresei/Adobe Stock Photo; p. 12 bc, p. 90 br, tl, p. 91 ct, cl, p. 96 tc, p. 97 cc, p. 133 bc © Sergey Peterman/Adobe Stock Photo; p. 12 br, p. 13 cc, p. 46 cc, p. 71 bc © Destina/Adobe Stock Photo; p. 13 tl, p. 13 cl, p. 71 tr, p. 133cr © Destina/Adobe Stock Photo; p. 13 tc © Kmit/Adobe Stock Photo; p. 13 tc © Nurbek/Adobe Stock Photo; p. 13 tr © Destina/Adobe Stock Photo; p. 13 cl © Destina/Adobe Stock Photo; p. 13 cc © Cobalt/Adobe Stock Photo; p. 13 cc © Maxim Kazmin/Adobe Stock Photo; p. 13 cr © Kmit/Adobe Stock Photo; p. 13 cl, cc © Arik/Adobe Stock Photo; p. 13 cc © Denis Rozhnovsky/Adobe Stock Photo; p. 13 cr, p. 39 br © Fatman 73/Adobe Stock Photo; p. 13 cc © Oleksandr Delyk/Adobe Stock Photo; p. 15 cl, p. 16 tl, p. 20 cl © Ion Popa/Adobe Stock Photo; p. 15 cc, p. 17 bc, p. 20 bl Mojang © 2009-2022. "Minecraft" is a trademark of Mojang AB; p. 15 cc, p. 16 tr © Used with permission from Ningbo Jus Internet Technology Co. Ltd.; p. 15 cr Zoom and the Zoom logo are trademarks of Zoom Video Communications, Inc.; p. 15 cl, p. 16 tc, p. 17 br, p. 20 cl, p. 40 cl, cr © Used with permission from Microsoft; p. 15 cr, p. 16 tc © Google™ search is a trademark of Google LLC. Google and Google Docs are trademarks of Google LLC and this book is not endorsed by or affiliated with Google in any way; p. 16 tc © Rahmawati Dian/Adobe Stock Photo; p. 17 cc © Google Classroom is a trademark of Google LLC. Google and Google Docs are trademarks of Google LLC and this book is not endorsed by or affiliated with Google in any way; p. 18 cl, p. 19 cl, p. 20 cl, p. 112 bc, p. 113 cl © Releon 8211/Adobe Stock Photo; p. 18 cr, p. 19 cl, p. 20 cc, p. 112 cc © Mkos 83/Adobe Stock Photo; p. 18 cl, p. 19 cl, p. 20 cl © ZMK Studio/Adobe Stock Photo; p. 18 cr © Norman Chan/Adobe Stock Photo; p. 19 cl, p. 20 cc © Maksym Yemelyanov/Adobe Stock Photo; p. 19 bl, p. 20 © Andrey Zyk/Adobe Stock Photo; p. 36 cl, p. 39 cc © Siberian Art/Adobe Stock Photo; p. 36 cc © Graphego/Adobe Stock Photo; p. 36 cr, p. 39 cr, p. 44 cr © Focus And Blur/Adobe Stock Photo; p. 36 cc, p. 39 cl, p. 46 tl, p. 136 cc © Scanrail/Adobe Stock Photo; p. 39 bl, p. 46 tr © Bergamont/Adobe Stock Photo; p. 39 bc, p. 44 cc © Epic Fantasy Maps/Adobe Stock Photo; p. 46 cl © Chonlasub/Adobe Stock Photo; p. 46 cl © Djomas/Adobe Stock Photo; p. 46 cl © Christian Musat/Adobe Stock Photo; p. 46 bc, p. 116 © Duncan Noakes/Adobe Stock Photo; p. 48 cc © Polat Alp/Adobe Stock Photo; p. 63 tr © Pictorial Press Ltd/Alamy Stock Photo; p. 65 cc © Ioan Panaite/Adobe Stock Photo; p. 66 tr, p. 80cc, p. 77 tl, tc, cl, cc, p. 80 tc, cc, cc, p. 81 tc, cr, cc, bc, p. 157 tr © Hachette UK; p. 67 tc © Shendart/Adobe Stock Photo; p. 67 cc © Rawpixel.com/Adobe Stock Photo; p. 68 tl © Toncsi/Adobe Stock Photo; p. 68 bl, p. 71 tl, cl, p. 133 cl, p. 141 cl © Avantgarde/Adobe Stock Photo; p. 69 br © BSD Studio/Adobe Stock Photo; p. 70 tr, p. 71 tc © Omnia/Adobe Stock Photo; p. 70 cl © Nerthuz/Adobe Stock Photo; p. 71 cl, p. 99 cc © Bisa 2 Bisa/Adobe Stock Photo; p. 71 cc, p. 99 cl, p. 133 cc, p. 136 cc © Pavel Sh/Adobe Stock Photo; p. 71 bl, p. 99 tl, p. 101 tl © Roman Milert/Adobe Stock Photo; p. 71 bc, p. 99 c © Handatko/Adobe Stock Photo; p. 71 cc, p. 133 cc, cl, p. 135 cc, p. 136 cl © New Africa/Adobe Stock Photo; p. 71 br © Aradelvalle Photo/Adobe Stock Photo; p. 72 cc © Vlad Kochelaevskiy/Adobe Stock Photo; p. 72 bc © Kharlamova lv/Adobe Stock Photo; p. 74 bc © Narathip 12/Adobe Stock Photo; p. 75 cr © Karin Hildebrand Lau/Alamy Stock Photo; p. 76 cc © Rawpixel.com/Adobe Stock Photo; p. 80 cc, cr © Igorkol Ter/Adobe Stock Photo; p. 87 br © Dule 964/Adobe Stock Photo; p. 88 cl, p. 92 cc © Ekostsov/Adobe Stock Photo; p. 88 cc, p. 92 bl © Taiyosun/Adobe Stock Photo; p. 88 cr, p. 96 tr, p. 97 cr, p. 98tc © Suradech/Adobe Stock Photo; p. 88 cc, p. 92 br, p. 97 bc, p. 99 tl © Sergiy 1975/Adobe Stock Photo; p. 88 cc, p. 92 cr, p. 97 br, p. 98 tc, p. 99 © Nosorogua/Adobe Stock Photo; p. 89 cr © Eveleen 007/Adobe Stock Photo; p. 90 cr, p. 91 cr, cl, br, p. 97 cc © Goir/Adobe Stock Photo; p. 90 cr, p. 91 cc, bc, p. 97 bl © Tech Stock Studio/Adobe Stock Photo; p. 93 cl © Alex/Adobe Stock Photo; p. 93 cc, p. 98 tc © Aliona Manakova/Adobe Stock Photo; p. 93 cr © Kuz Com/Adobe Stock Photo; p. 93 cc © Marcelo Trad Nery/Adobe Stock Photo; p. 93 cr © Vlabo/Adobe Stock Photo; p. 93 br, p. 97 cr, p. 101 cl © Silkstock/Adobe Stock Photo; p. 94 cc, p. 96tl © Julien Tromeur/Adobe Stock Photo; p. 94 bl © Vladislav Ociacia/Adobe Stock Photo; p. 94 br © DM7/Adobe Stock Photo; p. 95 tl, p. 98 cr, p. 157 br © Phonlamai Photo/Adobe Stock Photo; p. 95 tr © Eplisterra/Adobe Stock Photo; p. 95 bl, p. 98 br © Tryfonov/Adobe Stock Photo; p. 95 br, p. 156 tc © Alexander Limbach/Adobe Stock Photo; p. 97 cl © And Sus/Adobe Stock Photo; p. 98 cl © Smole/Adobe Stock Photo; p. 98 bl © Unlimit3d/Adobe Stock Photo; p. 101 tr © Sevulya/Adobe Stock Photo; p. 101 cl © Jnsepeliova/Adobe Stock Photo; p. 101 cr © Imagedb.com/Adobe Stock Photo; p. 107 br, p. 114 cr, p. 115 cc © Google Forms is a trademark of Google LLC. Google and Google Docs are trademarks of Google LLC and this book is not endorsed by or affiliated with Google in any way; p. 113 cl © Mipan/Adobe Stock Photo; p. 113 cl © New Africa/Adobe Stock Photo; p. 113 bl © Sommai/Adobe Stock Photo; p. 116 cl © Voren 1/Adobe Stock Photo; p. 116 cl © Gallinago Media/Adobe Stock Photo; p. 116 cl © Esvetleishaya/Adobe Stock Photo; p. 116 cl © Eric Isselée/Adobe Stock Photo; p. 116 cl © Ksena 32/Adobe Stock Photo; p. 117 cc © Ray Massey/Getty Images; p. 118 cl © Thanawong/Adobe Stock Photo; p. 118 cr © Vlasdv/Adobe Stock Photo; p. 118 cc © Happy Vector 071/Adobe Stock Photo; p. 118 cr © 103 tnn/Adobe Stock Photo; p. 129 cr © Interfoto/Alamy Stock Photo; p. 131 cl © Illustrez-vous/Adobe Stock Photo; p. 131 cr © Jon Le-Bon/Adobe Stock Photo; p. 133 cr © AVD/Adobe Stock Photo; p. 135 cr, p. 140 cc © Aleksey Boldin/Alamy Stock Photo; p. 135 cr © Kamil Majdański/Alamy Stock Photo; p. 136 cr © Splitov 27/Adobe Stock Photo; p. 137 cc, p. 139 cc © Terovesalainen/Adobe Stock Photo; p. 148 cc, p. 149 cc, p. 150 cc, p. 151 tr, p. 152 cc, p. 154 cc, p. 155 © Kup 1984/Adobe Stock Photo; p. 155 cl © Sergii Moscaliuk/Adobe Stock Photo; p. 155 cl © PF Images/Adobe Stock Photo; p. 155 cc © Dragana/Adobe Stock Photo; p. 155 cc © Rolandas/Adobe Stock Photo; p. 155 cc © Sdecoret/Adobe Stock Photo; p. 155 cr © Elenathewise/Adobe Stock Photo.

t = top, *b* = bottom, *l* = left, *r* = right, *c* = centre